Sinop Landscapes

Sinop Landscapes

Exploring Connection in a Black Sea Hinterland

Owen P. Doonan

UNIVERSITY OF PENNSYLVANIA MUSEUM

of Archaeology and Anthropology

Philadelphia

ISBN 1-931707-65-0

Library of Congress Cataloging-in-Publication Data

Doonan, Owen P.
 Sinop landscapes : exploring connection in a Black Sea hinterland / Owen P.
Doonan.-- 1st ed.
    p. cm.
 Includes bibliographical references and index.
 ISBN 1-931707-65-0 (alk. paper)
 1. Sinop (Turkey)--Antiquities 2. Sinop (Turkey)--History. I. Title.
 DS156.S6D66 2004
 939'.31--dc22
                                        2004001994

About the Author

Owen Doonan is Assistant Professor of Art History at California State
University Northridge and a Research Associate in the Near Eastern
Section of the University of Pennsylvania Museum of Archaeology and
Anthropology, Philadelphia. He is Director of the Sinop Regional
Archaeological Project and co-editor of *The Dictionary of Black Sea
Antiquities* (forthcoming).

Printed in the United States of America on acid-free paper

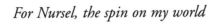

For Nursel, the spin on my world

Contents

Figures

Tables

Foreword

Prehistoric remains on hilltops, early churches draped with thick vegetation, walls of ancient towns submerged along the coast, intact ships found in the deep anoxic seawaters—all of these features are tantalizing evidence of a rich culture history along the Turkish Black Sea coast.

This volume offers the first overview of one of the most important coastal regions of the Black Sea: the isolated peninsula of Sinop, Turkey. The port of Sinop is the northernmost point of Anatolia, located on a forested plain jutting into the Black Sea, practically an island along the coast. The peninsula is surrounded on three sides by the sea and cut off from Anatolia's inland cultures by the steep and forbidding Pontic Mountains.

The Sinop peninsula was populated and prosperous for the last 10 millennia. Sinop's cultural connections and history of occupation are closely linked to the maritime orientation of the coastal Black Sea world. Part of a system of ports and hinterlands whose primary markets were with other coastal centers, Sinop thus serves as a pulse point for the waxing and waning of maritime economies around the Black Sea.

This peninsula was chosen in 1994 as the launching point for an integrated land and sea program designed to investigate the archaeological landscape along the coast, in shallow water and in deep water. The Black Sea Trade Project created a coordinated map of archaeological remains, including the hinterland and port, the traces of the boats that plied these waters, and the cargoes of the vessels. Research design for both land and under water needed to be modified to produce comparable data. On land, the program used a systematic sampling strategy that mimicked the back-and-forth mapping of underwater sonar and made an effort to map various environments that could be carried into the sea in a "mountaintop to ocean bottom" transect. Underwater surveys were carried out during the same period.

Doonan's volume presents the results of the land survey on the Sinop peninsula—a study of a coastal world that developed and evolved in relationship to the sea, focusing on the hinterland behind the port of Sinop. The lands that provided its subsistence are surprisingly diverse in their topography and resources. The survey mapped lithics and ceramic scatters and architectural features which allows for a reconstruction of changing land use over time and documents the emergence of an economy oriented to the sea. The study of the settlement of the peninsula provides both a cultural baseline for the history of the port itself and a baseline for the broader integration of archaeological remains along the coast on land and under water.

Fredrik T. Hiebert, Director
Black Sea Trade Project
National Geographic Society

Preface

This volume presents a perspective on the results we have obtained through the Sinop Regional Archaeological Project to date, synthesizing that work through the filter of other research that has been carried out in the region. This is not meant to be a final or even an interim report but an exploration of where an ongoing project stands. I invoke the metaphors of walking and exploring because perspectives emerge as part of active and ongoing process; they don't spring fully formed from hard drives and data bases.

The Sinop promontory is rich in diverse places, each a confluence of geography, culture, and history that has distinctive qualities. In a region like this it is easy to think of the places as special and worthy of note. Writing a totalizing history of Sinop promontory seems impossible unless we choose to prioritize the importance of a single perspective, most likely leaving the hinterland as a darkened backdrop to the history of a vibrant port. Places are confluences rather than points and so do not have sharp edges, but build up over time and gain significance through relationships emerging in time and space. Movement, connection, dynamic interaction between inhabitants and inhabited all create the places that are the subject of this volume.

Like places, no project ever stands by itself alone. The production and publication of information that can be used and evaluated by others is critical to any investigation. As we continue to conduct research in and about Sinop we will be bringing out results in a variety of media that can connect our colleagues to our data. The data created by research must be reliable and sufficient to support interpretation. At times in the book I advocate a more integrated approach to "heads up" (extensive/experiential) and "heads down" (systematic/analytical) survey. This is by no means a call to distract investigators from doing reliable systematic survey that gets results that can be compared to those obtained elsewhere. In fact, I hope this volume offers a strong case for more analytical approaches in certain regions where exceptional coverage in non-systematic methods have created outstanding opportunities for focused systematic work.

When considering the debts to family, friends, and colleagues I have incurred in producing this volume I feel more like I have presided over a potlach than withdrawn into the solitary solipsism of academic writing. First, I would like to thank my collaborators at the Sinop Regional Archaeological Project (SRAP) whose efforts as much as mine have produced the results discussed in this book. Fred Hiebert, Director of the Black Sea Trade Project (BSTP), has encouraged me with tireless support and innumerable ideas that are difficult to separate from my own. SRAP is the terrestrial component of BSTP, a multidisciplinary research program that investigates contact and culture formation around the Black Sea in terrestrial and maritime environments (Hiebert et al. 1997). Alex Gantos, Assistant Director of the survey, contributed greatly to my thinking about the landscapes of Sinop and has made particularly important contributions to fieldwork design, mapping and landscape interpretation, the heart of a survey project. Most of the maps of places in the Sinop promontory in this volume have been based on his original drawings.

David Smart initially got our group together—his initiative and persistence were instrumental in luring me away from the west Mediterranean to work in the Black Sea. Randy Olson generously allowed me to reproduce several of his photographs from his Black Sea expedition in 2000. The many students and other team members of BSTP have contributed so much to the work that is discussed here, I thank them for their patience and hard work.

Professor Jeremy A. Sabloff, the Williams Director of the University of Pennsylvania Museum, has been a valuable and unstinting supporter of the project and this publication from the start. Among the many faculty and students at Penn who have made suggestions or contributed ideas I would like to single out Clark Erickson for his valuable discussions of landscape archaeology, David Romano for stimulating discussions on classical and post-classical landscapes, and Keith DeVries, whose experience in Turkey and insights into Anatolian culture have been so helpful.

Richard Saller, Provost of the University of Chicago, and John Ramsey, Chair of the Department of Classics at University of Illinois-Chicago, both supported the project during my years in Chicago during which the fieldwork presented here was accomplished. Jim Smith, Head of the Division of Social Sciences, Penn State, Abington supported the final stages of writing and provided computer equipment without which much of the image processing and analysis would have been impossible.

My colleagues in the Black Sea, both in Turkey and around the shores, have given new meaning to the term "Hospitable Sea." Gocha Tsetskhladze has provided extensive advice on many issues and helped me to obtain difficult-to-access materials. Sergey Solovyov, Marina Vakhtina, and Denis Zhuravlev were helpful and informative hosts during visits to the State Hermitage Museum and the State Historical Museum. Otar Lordkipanidze and the staff of the Institute of Archaeology, Georgian Academy of Sciences, have shown extraordinary hospitality on several research visits. His recent death was a great blow to Black Sea archaeology. Guram Kvirkveliya introduced me to many of the exciting ongoing archaeological investigations in Georgia.

The Directors of the Sinop Museum—Ismail Tatlican (up to 2000) and Musa Özcan (2001 and ongoing)—Researchers Fuat Dereli and Hale Özan, and the museum staff have facilitated our work in far too many ways to recount here. Many friends in and around Sinop have helped in many ways, but particular thanks are due to Atilla Ayyildiz for technical and logistical support.

The General Directorate for Monuments and Museums, Ministry of Culture, Turkey, granted permission to carry out the 1996–1999 field seasons. Thanks go to General Directors M. A. Isik, Professor Dr. Ender Varinlioglu, Kenan Yurttagul, and Dr. Alpay Pasinli for their permission and support. Our representatives from the Turkish Ministry of Culture have been exemplary in their patience, helpfulness, and professionalism: Cevdet Sevinç, Elmas Kaya, Sena Mutlu, and Nurhan Turan.

Many colleagues in Turkey and abroad have generously offered assistance and support of various kinds: Berna Alpagut, Önder Bilgi, Joe Carter, Jim Dengate, Ugur Dogan, Sevket Dönmez, Hugh Elton, Stephen Hill, R. Ross Holloway, Yvon Garlan, Charles and Marie-Henriette Gates, Andrew Goldman, Martha Joukowsky, Dominique Kassab-Tezgör, Hans Lohmann, Roger Matthews, Jacques Morin, Mehmet Özdogan, Ilknur Özgen, Eyup Özveren, Nick Rauh, Maya Vassileva, Volkmar von Graeve, LuAnn Wandsnider, Tony Wilkinson, and Rolf Winkes. Toni Cross, former Director of the Ankara branch of the American Research Institute in Turkey, built ARIT Ankara into a vital and productive research center, a critical resource for all of us working in Turkey. She is missed by all of us working in Anatolia.

Several patient colleagues have saved me from many errors of fact and interpretation by critiquing drafts of parts or all of the book: Alex

Bauer, Fred Hiebert, Chris Lightfoot, Eyup Özveren, Nick Rauh, and Tony Wilkinson. The efforts of these colleagues have improved the book greatly. Walda Metcalf and James R. Mathieu at the University of Pennsylvania Museum Publications have shepherded this from manuscript to volume and I sincerely appreciate their efforts. Responsibility for those errors that remain belongs to me.

Funding for the fieldwork was provided by the National Geographic Foundation, the Samuel S. Freeman Charitable Trusts, and private donors. Funding for preparing the manuscript for publication was provided by the Robert S. Dyson, Jr., Fellowship in Near Eastern Archaeology at the University of Pennsylvania Museum (1999–2001), the International Research Exchanges Board (IREg), and an ARIT-NEH Fellowship (1999–2000).

My final and deepest debts are to the family and friends who have provided unstinting support and patience during the writing of this volume. Jay Shaughnessy and Bahar Ceceli provided good cheer and a place to stay during transitional difficulties. I thank my parents Mary and Owen Doonan, my siblings, and other close family for their patience with a missing son, brother and uncle. Annemiz Mükrime Uçkan fed and sheltered us on extended trips to Ankara. And most of all, canim Nurum, sözlerim yeterli degil. It is to you I dedicate this book.

Chronology

Timeline of Major Archaeological Periods, Evidence, and Cultural Trends on the Sinop Promontory.

Period	Dates	Cultural Trends and Major Sites
Neolithic	ca. 8000–4000 BCE	Pre-ceramic settlement at Inceburun, proposed flood (Ryan and Pittman 1997), ceramic Neolithic shows parallels to sites near the sea of Marmara [Mezarlıktepe]
Chalcolithic	ca. 4000–2700 BCE	[Maltepe]
Early Bronze	ca. 2700–2000 BCE	Widespread settlement in Sinop [Kocagöz] and Samsun (e.g., Ikiztepe) regions; limited parallels on Sinop [Gulluavlu] to Karanova (Bulgaria), Troy (NW Anatolia), and Catacomb culture (Ukraine)
Middle-Late Bronze	ca. 2000–1000 BCE	Limited contacts with central Anatolia [Gulluavlu], Kashka tribes from central Black Sea Anatolia mentioned in Hittite sources
Iron	ca. 1000–600 BCE	Establishment of coastal settlements [Köşk höyük-Gerze, Sinop kale NW, Fener-Akliman], clear connections between Sinop port and north Black Sea [Sinop kale NW]
Archaic	7th–early 5th c. BCE	Foundation of Sinope by Miletus and Sinopean colonies in the east Black Sea
Classical	5th–4th c. BCE	Foundation of Athenian cleruchy (colony) at Sinope (430s), Xenophon and the Ten Thousand pass through Sinope/Harmene (400), Datames's seige of Sinope (ca. 368), mass production of Sinope amphoras for distribution around the Black Sea (ca. 360– onward BCE)
Hellenistic	4th–early 1st c. BCE	Capture of Sinope by Pharnaces I, Sinope made capital of the Pontic Kingdom (183), expansion of coastal settlement [Keçioğlu-Demirci], expansion and strengthening of the city walls, wars against Rome (early 1st c. BCE)

[/] Sites from Sinop discussed in the text are bracketed.

Timeline of Major Archaeological Periods, Evidence, and Cultural Trends on the Sinop Promontory.

Period	Dates	Cultural Trends and Major Sites
Roman	early 1st c. BCE – 3rd c. CE	Conquest of Sinope by Lucullus (70 BCE), Roman colony Colonia Iulia Felix Sinope (46 BCE), prosperous agricultural villas in the hinterland [Karapınar]
Late Roman/ Early Byzantine	4th–7th c. CE	Widespread agricultural industry Demirci], expansion of suburban settlement [Kiraztepe], extensive building of churches in the hinterland [Çiftlik, Gerna, Kuz (Erfelek)]
Middle-Late Byzantine	8th–13th c. CE	Arab invasions (830s–850s), Turkish invasion under Karatekin (1081), struggle between Byzantium and Trebizond for control of the central Black Sea, declining hinterland settlement
Seljuk	13th–15th c. CE	Extensive repair of the city walls and public building in Sinop town; isolation of the port from the hinterland [Pervane medrese, Alaattin mosque]
Ottoman	15th–20th c. CE	Conquest by Mehmet II (1461), increased shipbuilding following the battle of Lepanto (1570), Cossack sack of Sinop (1614), Russian sack of Sinop (1853), slow recovery of the town and hinterland (later 19th c.)
Republican	1923–to date	Exchange of populations (1920s), expansion of agriculture along south coast (1920s–50s), extensive road building, establishment of district capital at Erfelek (1961), U.S.–Turkish military base on Boztepe (1960s–90s), suburban and industrial expansion on Boztepe and along the coast south of Sinop (1950s–), dependence of hinterland economy on contributions from relatives in Turkish and foreign cities

[/] Sites from Sinop discussed in the text are bracketed.

1

The Sinop Hinterland

Exploring Connection around the Black Sea

Looking north from the windy height of Boztepe you can peer far into the mists of the Black Sea with no land in sight (Figures 1-1 and 1-2). When a storm comes up from the west, you might make out a few dolphins skimming alongside the small craft racing around Boztepe to port in the inky blackness of the sea. Beneath your feet the modern town of Sinop (Greek and Roman Sinope) sprawls up the slopes of Boztepe just as its Ottoman and Seljuk Turkish, Byzantine, Roman, and Greek predecessor has done for 2,600 years (Figure 1-3). The Greeks from Miletus named this town Sinope when they founded a colony here in the late 7th century BCE. From now on the name Sinope will be used to refer to the port during Greco-Roman times and the name Sinop will refer to the port at other times and the promontory in all periods.

Turning around to the south the far horizon is pierced by the rugged Pontic mountains that rise up behind the port of Gerze, about 25 km distant by sea and 40 by land (Figure 1-4). The green rolling hills of the Sinop promontory, a patchwork of forests and farms, spread out between the town and the mountains (Figure 1-5). In the harbor below colorful fishing boats and gray merchant ships lay at anchor waiting out the infamous squalls that led Greek colonists to call this the "Inhospitable Sea" (Pontus Axeinus) when they first encountered it. Dangerous storms, unfriendly inhabitants of the coasts and the interior, and the total absence of the islands and ports that made their native Aegean so easy to navigate made the Greeks' first impressions unfavorable.

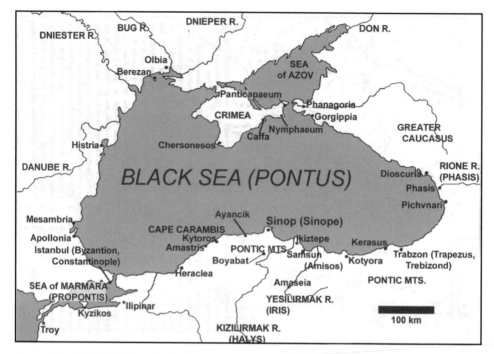

Figure 1-1: The Black Sea, indicating places named in the text. Sinop/Sinope is located at the tip of the promontory protruding into the Black Sea at the center of the Turkish coast.

The Greeks renamed the Black Sea the "Hospitable Sea" (Pontus Euxinus) after they had colonized a necklace of places along it, creating a suitably linked arena for trade and communications (Figure 1-1). Colonization is a process situated in the living spaces, literatures, and minds of colonizers and colonized. It is also a process of claiming, taming, and transforming human landscapes (Deetz 1990; Dougherty 1993). Over time relationships become naturalized, balancing linkages and ruptures between communities that perceive the world in different ways. In the end these relationships can develop a stability that transcends particular moments in politics and history. This book is an exploration of the linkage of the port of Sinop on the Pontic coast of Turkey with its diverse hinterland and greater Black Sea–Eurasian worlds.

The relationship of the port to its hinterland plays out at many temporal and geographical scales. At some times and places local institutions and practices enhanced inhabitants' feeling of connectedness with other parts of their world (Horden and Purcell 2000). These institutions

Figure 1-2: The town of Sinop has been set on the sandy isthmus connecting the headland of Boztepe to the coast of the mainland since the 7th century BCE. Greek colonists from Miletus named this port Sinope, which remained its name until the Turkish conquests in the 13th century CE.

might or might not have encouraged political identification with Sinop port itself, and at some times they were entangled with larger systems. Connections could be economic, political, ideological, technological, and/ or religious. In some times and places these were a strong feature of daily life and at others they were not.

In the Sinop region connectedness can most easily be traced along economic and social lines. Economic linkages can be understood through the integrated processes of consumption and production. Archaeological surveys rely primarily on modifications to the landscape and the distribution of abandoned or discarded refuse to identify the nature of human activities in a place. Heavy concentrations of burned debris or storage vessels can identify an industrial area. Construction materials and pottery associated with eating and drinking might mark the position of a house. Mounded tumuli or fragments of building tiles mixed with human bones show where there was a cemetery. By record-

Figure 1-3: Late 19th century woodcut print of the town of Sinop and the mainland from Boztepe.

ing places like these in the landscape we can piece together the patterns of life in the past. Looking at how those patterns are distributed in different kinds of places helps us understand the choices people made about interacting with each other and their environment. Connections between people in different places can be traced by observing consumption of durable materials from known producers and can suggest linkages between the producers and consumers. On the other hand the nature of these linkages is not always easy to determine.

Why study connection? Connection is fundamental to the creation and maintenance of culture. It is a mutual dependency between people separated by time or space. Connection binds people together through social, economic, and ideological habits and practices. Social connection establishes relationships between and within communities. Economic connection develops the different potentials of various ecological and topographic situations to create a specialized system of production and consumption. Ideological connection naturalizes the ties that bind people to places and to people in other places. Political, religious, and cul-

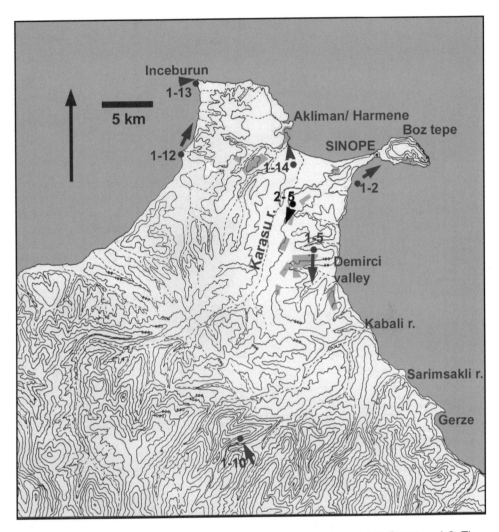

Figure 1-4: Map of Sinop promontory showing the places mentioned in Chapters 1-2. The locations and orientations of Figures 1-2, 1-5, 1-10, 1-12, 1-13, 1-14, and 2-9 are indicated.

tural practices and institutions maintain these connections. Physical and organizational infrastructure strengthens them: land ownership regulations, road systems, port facilities, fortifications.

The political configuration of the promontory and in particular its relationship with the port at Sinope has varied considerably over the past 5,000 years. These relationships are particularly sensitive to the rhythms

Figure 1-5: A landscape panorama from the Demirci ridge to the south promontory. Visible in the foreground are the fertile agricultural fields typical of the east coast of the promontory. The coast is visible to the east (left side) and the rolling hills of the outer promontory to the west (right side). The mountains behind Gerze loom in the distance.

of political and economic organization in the Black Sea. At times the Black Sea regional economy was strongly interdependent. Close economic and political coordination between the north and south coasts encouraged specialized production and the Sinop hinterland became actively engaged in Black Sea culture and exchange. At other times political rivalries highlighted the strategic importance of Sinop port as a point for controlling east-west Black Sea communications. At these times the Sinop hinterland became less engaged in regional politics and economy.

In general, those times when a north-south axis of trade was important (Hellenistic, Roman, emerging post-Soviet) the ecological distinctiveness of the Sinop promontory was highlighted and the promontory became strongly engaged in the regional trade system. In times when the east-west axis was critical (early Greek colonial, late Byzantine–early modern) the promontory's distinctive ecology was less significant and the hinterland withdrew from regional systems. In such times the strategic importance of the port was critical to the military, political, and/ or economic systems around the Black Sea.

We live in an era of unprecedented connectedness, so it is easy to take this idea for granted. Today in the conservative mountain villages of Sinop connectedness is maintained through *yayla* (highland pasture) festivals (Figure 1-6) and the critical economic contributions and extended annual visits paid by relatives from such distant cities as Sinop, Ankara, Istanbul, and Amsterdam (Meeker 2000; Beller-Hann and Hann 2001). In July and August it is not at all rare to see a brand new BMW negotiating the dizzying mountain village roads, never paved but at least dry in summer.

Figure 1-6: A Circassian *yayla* (highland pasture) festival in the highlands of Sinop. Participants come from Sinop, Samsun, Istanbul, and Europe to reaffirm kinship and cultural bonds. A dance teacher has come from Ingushetia in the Caucasus mountains northeast of the Black Sea to lead the group in traditional dances.

The perception of connectedness is the essence of what we are exploring in the Black Sea Trade Project (BSTP): how connected did people feel to those in other upland villages, coastal villages, and ports, the big port of Sinop or to distant shores: the Crimea, Istanbul, Rome? At those times when connections were strong, how did religious, economic, infrastructural, political, and ethnic institutions bind local populations to larger systems, and how were these various institutional processes situated in landscapes?

The Pontic coast is different from the rest of Turkey. For more than 5,000 years this coast has been connected to the cultures and economies of the Black Sea, at times seeming more remote from the rest of the Anatolian land mass than Greece, Italy, or Africa. For many in Anatolia the Pontic coast was an overseas destination. Before the introduction of dynamite most travelers in the region crossed from the central Anatolian

Figure 1-7: The corridor of the Kizilirmak River cutting through the Pontic mountains south of Samsun. The winding, steep-sided canyon makes high-volume traffic and long-distance trade difficult.

plateau to the coast at Trabzon or in the western part of the region where the mountain crossings are easier. The most suitable crossing through the Pontic mountains is via the valley of the Kizilirmak (ancient Halys) river, which is not particularly suitable for high-volume long-distance trade (Figure 1-7). Sinop occupied the central point on the coast, a couple days by sea from either outlet.

Crossing the mountains was difficult and dangerous for outsiders, as a group of Polish merchants learned in 1576/77 when they attempted to cross the mountains south of Sinope on the road to Aleppo. They were set upon and killed by a group of students from a medrese, a religious school, in Sinop in collaboration with local authorities and merchants in five different towns spread over hundreds of km.

Communications could be easy or difficult, depending on who you were and what you were trying to transport (Faroqhi 1984:66-69). Poorly

Figure 1-8: The infamous weather and topography of the Pontic highlands has frustrated travelers for millennia (courtesy of R. Olson).

defined tracks, dizzying valleys, and unpredictable weather make the Pontic mountains treacherous even in the best of seasons (Figure 1-8).

The Pontic mountains are more than just a physical barrier to traffic between the coast and plateau. The people and environment on either side are fundamentally different too. Even today, many of the coastal inhabitants see their inland neighbors as conservative and backward, while those who dwell inland see the coast as populated by unbelievers and scoundrels. The climate north of the Pontic watershed is moist and mild in contrast to arid continental conditions inland. Fish, arboreal fruits and nuts, and small farms feed the coastal populations, while large-scale cereal farming dominates in the valleys south of the Pontic watershed (Tarkan 1941). For the past 5,000 years the people of the inland valleys along the north Anatolian fault have belonged to the cultures of central Anatolia. On the other hand, communities along the coast and in the valleys that run from the Pontic watershed to the coast have participated in the Black Sea world, closer to their overseas neighbors in the Crimea and the Caucasus than to those 30 km to their south.

There are few extensive coastal plains on the south coast of the Black Sea capable of supporting large populations: the Kizilirmak and Yesilirmak (ancient Iris) deltas and the Sinop promontory. The two great river deltas are extensive plains with monotonously uniform topography, while the Sinop promontory is characterized by profuse diversity. Since the Bronze Age Sinop's port, coast, and hinterland have formed an interface for a succession of maritime, lowland and mountain cultures. These communities did not always connect with one another despite their physical proximity.

Sinop has been a critical node in the communications, production, exchange, and political systems of the Black Sea from as early as 2500 BCE onward (Hiebert et al. 1997b). The port commands the best natural landing on the entire Pontic Anatolian coast. While building a girls' school on the slopes of Boztepe in the 1970s workmen uncovered a Bronze Age burial tumulus with bronze daggers showing clear connections to the eastern Black Sea (Isin 1989). In 2000 members of our team excavated a precolonial settlement at the port of Sinop that showed close connections to the cultures of coastal Ukraine and the Crimea (Hiebert et al. forthcoming; see Chapter 3). The Greek-local relationship does not seem to have been close at the time when colonists from Miletus arrived to found Sinope (around 630 BCE; see Chapter 4). Over the next 2,500 years Athenians, Romans, Genoese, Circassians, Turks, and countless others have settled in Sinop and its hinterland, creating a diverse community with extensive overseas links.

The promontory owes its importance for maritime communications to its situation in the Black Sea. Inceburun on the west coast is the northernmost point in Anatolia. The circulation of surface currents in the eastern and western lobes of the Black Sea assists sailors departing across to the Crimea and coming back (Hiebert et al. 1997). Boztepe and the eastern side of the promontory provides shelter from the fierce storms of the Black Sea for ships sailing along the long rocky south coast. Thus Sinop has great potential to control north-south and east-west traffic in the Black Sea.

The distinctive pottery of Sinope peppered with black sand inclusions has been found in astonishing abundance at sites particularly along the north and west coasts (Fedoseyev 1992; Monochov 1993; Conovici 1998; De Boer forthcoming). This distinctive pottery, particularly the trade amphoras used to transport bulk commodities, indicates intensive trade. In contrast, few Sinopean ceramics appear south of the mountains, suggesting limited trade relationships.

The close relationship of Sinope to the north coast is hardly surprising. The lower river valleys of the Don, Dniepr, Dniester, Bug, and Danube have extensive fertile plains and the dry steppe climate ideal for cereal cultivation. The rich grain fields of the north coast comprised one of the great breadbaskets of the ancient Black Sea and Mediterranean worlds. Sinope on the other hand, was one of the few parts of the Black Sea where the climate favored olive cultivation. These staples formed the backbone of a complex trade relationship between the two coasts that lasted more than a thousand years (ca. 400 BCE - 600 CE). Nearly a thousand years later the customs registers from Caffa in the Crimea demonstrate the continuation of this close relationship (Inalcik 1995).

The north-south axis of economic and cultural interaction was identified as a critical structure in the Black Sea's long-term development by the Romanian historian Bratianu (1969) in his structural history of the Black Sea (see also Özveren 2001). He argued that over the past several thousand years the Black Sea has functioned as a *placque tournant* ["turntable"] around which the empires and economies of the Eurasian Steppe, the Mediterranean, and the Middle East have revolved (Bratianu 1969:43). The Black Sea is the arena in which the people of these distinctive regions have clashed and cooperated for millennia. Sinop, the pivot of Black Sea communications, mediated the economic and political relationships of these wider cultural and economic regions.

The cultural diversity of the Black Sea coasts and the wealth and political strength of the polities on its various shores have had a centripetal effect on political authority in the region. The most effective imperial regimes have exercised economic rather than political or military power, established through control of traffic between the region and outside markets. Constantinople-Istanbul is the most notable example of an imperial capital based on this strategy, but to a lesser extent the Cimmerian bosphorus and the passes behind Trabzon have enriched local kingdoms in a similar manner. Since the 7th century BCE a series of outsiders (e.g., Milesian, Genoese, Rhum, Armenian) has inserted agents into cities and towns along the coasts, each creating a highly effective trade diaspora (Stein 1999). Wealth was created and power balances maintained through a careful architecture of agreements, rivalries, and mutual dependencies in a classic heterarchical power structure (Crumley 1995). Sinop port and hinterland were highly attuned to the rhythms of coherence and disintegration, making it an ideal location to study the formation and synthesis of Black Sea cultures and economies over the past 5,000 years.

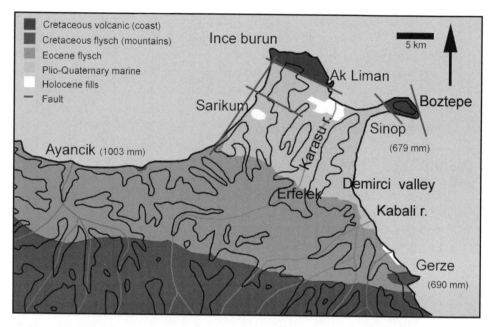

Figure 1-9: The major geological regions of Sinop promontory, including the outer volcanic, the central mixed marine, and highland flysch zones. Major faults are marked with thin straight lines. Primary faults occur where the Cretaceous volcanic bedrock has thrust up above the later (Neogene) mixed marine deposits and along the west coast where the promontory has thrust up with respect to the sea bed. Severe folding in the highlands has produced the dramatic relief apparent in the topography. Rainfall is indicated at Ayancik, Sinop, and Gerze in mm/annum.

This book foregrounds the importance of distinctive places on the Sinop promontory. Places are more than locations—a place is the intersection of physical, topographic, and human contexts (see Horden and Purcell 2000:77-80). Places acquire meaning through human perceptions of physical, geographic, ecological, historical, cultural and social features. A brief description of the physical features that give form to the diverse places of Sinop promontory includes the following: roughly 25 x 25 km in extent, the complex and dynamic geology, geomorphology, and climate of the promontory create an ecological region particularly rich in plant and animal resources. The coast itself is also diverse, varying between forbidding volcanic cliffs and small valleys with easy landings. The hinterland includes rolling hills suitable for agriculture, impassable forested mountain gorges, and highland plateaus offering easy communications, rich pasturage, and fertile agricultural fields.

Table 1-1: Formation of Sinop Promontory, Summary of Chronological Periods

Period	Dates	Characteristics
Upper Cretaceous	144–66.4 MY	Flysch formations in Pontic mountains; volcanic formations at Inceburun and Boztepe
Eocene	57.8–36.6 MY	Flysch formations in highlands at and above Erfelek and Kabali
Miocene	23.7–5.3 MY	Limestone caps form on Boztepe and Inceburun; Boztepe thrust 200 m and Inceburun 100 m upward by tectonic action
Pliocene	5.3–1.8 MY	Sandy-marly deposits form on the middle elevations (up to ca. 200 m asl) of Sinop promontory
Quaternary	1.8 MY–present	Shallow marine deposits form over most of Sinop coastal plain, including isthmus connecting Boztepe to mainland
Holocene	11,000–present	Alluvial filling of the Karasu delta and other river basins; Black Sea inundation

All dates before present; MY = million years.

The Sinop promontory is composed of four main geological zones (Figure 1-9; Table 1-1). The high mountains run east-west in a thick belt of Upper Cretaceous flysch, a sedimentary rock formed as steep mountains erode into the sea (Ketin 1961, Akkan 1975). These rise above 1,700 m at Zindan Dagi (1730 m) in the mountains south of Ayancik (Tarkan 1941: 7; Sinop Valiligi 2002). The primary rivers of the promontory flow off this watershed: the Karasu çayi, Kabali çayi, and the Sarimsakli çayi. The bedrock in this zone is severely folded and dramatically eroded, with all but impassable gorges separating forested ridges. This zone receives the highest levels of rainfall in Sinop province, resulting in devastating seasonal flooding that washes away roads, bridges, and even villages.

A belt of Eocene flysch runs from just west of Ayancik to Gerze, bordered on the north by the Kabali çayi alluvial zone and an anticlinal fault running northwest-southeast on the southwestern side of the promontory. The topography of the two flysch zones is similar, with severe folding creating dramatic and nearly impassable valleys and upland plateaus (Figure 1-10). Beneath the treeline the two regions are similar in ecological terms as well.

Figure 1-10: Landscape in the highland flysch zone showing exposed deformed folded bedrock near the center of the photograph and the generally rough topography typical of the highlands. The mound at the center of the photograph is the precolonial settlement of Maltepe (Tepealti).

The modern town of Erfelek sits on the Karasu river just above the transition between the highland flysch zone and the rolling hills typical of the coastal plain, formed on mixed Plio-Quaternary marine deposits. These deposits consist of mixed sandstones, marls, and occasional limestone outcrops. During the Holocene longshore transport of sandy sediments closed off the Karasu delta, formerly an embayment opening onto the north coast between the Inceburun and Boztepe volcanic masses (Figure 1-11; Besonen in Doonan et al. 2001). Wind-transported sands closed off another embayment opening onto the west coast forming the Sarikum lake (Akkan 1975: 56). The Sarikum depression was formed by an east-west fault to the north. A second fault runs southwest-northeast, defining the western shore of the promontory (Figure 1-12).

The extreme north of the Sinop promontory is defined by two Cretaceous volcanic masses: Boztepe and Inceburun (Figure 1-13; Akkan 1974:31-44). At the time of their formation these two were part

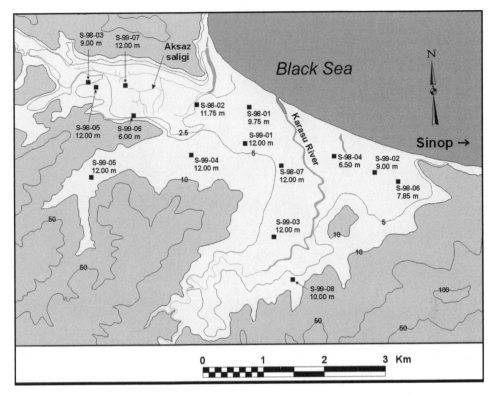

Figure 1-11: Map of the Karasu delta showing the shorelines of the mid-Holocene embayment and the extent to which the colluvial delta has filled in. The locations are indicated of sample cores taken as part of the survey's geomorphological study.

of the same volcanic mass, but after the Miocene period tectonic action thrust Boztepe 200 m higher while the Inceburun volcanic mass was pushed up only about 50 m. Both volcanic masses formed under the sea, based on the layers of marls inter-bedded with mixed volcanic rocks. On Boztepe the volcanic deposits included the pyroxene "black sand" used as temper in Sinope's signature transport amphora production in Greek and Roman times.

Boztepe and the southern edge of the Inceburun volcanics are both topped by Miocene fossiliferous limestone caps that demonstrate the submergence of these two areas about 20 million years ago. Pliocene-Quaternary shallow marine sediments have built up against the limestone cap at the southern edge of the volcanic zone on the west coast about 5 km south of Inceburun, covering the older deposits. A fault runs

Figure 1-12: The west coast of Sinop promontory looking north from Sarikum toward Inceburun. The soft sandstone cliffs alternate with small coastal valleys along this coast.

west-east 5 km south of Inceburun through the Akliman harbor, where the bedrock to the south has dropped down relative to the rising volcanic mass. The two small islands in Akliman harbor illustrate the transition between the northern volcanic mass and the southern mixed marine sediments (Figure 1-14). The northern Black island (Karaada, also called Fener after the lighthouse on it) is composed of volcanic rock, and the southern Yellow island (Sariada) is sandstone.

A series of valleys opens onto the coasts of the Sinop promontory, carved by tectonic action and erosion. Several of these have been filled in with eroded soils during the Holocene period. Deposits of clay are plentiful on several of these valley floors where marly deposits have been eroded. These clays have been used extensively for production of ceramics and construction material, particularly in the Demirci valley, where the clays are mixed with fine pyroxene deposits (Kuzucuoglu and Andrieu 1998; Kassab and Tatlican 1998).

The Sinop promontory's formation has created diverse local microenvironments which are widely dispersed across the entire land mass.

Figure 1-13: Cretaceous volcanic formation at Inceburun, the northernmost point in Anatolia. The pre-ceramic Paleolithic and Neolithic remains here provided the earliest evidence documented to date for human occupation in Sinop promontory.

Mineral resources are more or less widely distributed with the exception of those associated with the Inceburun and Boztepe volcanic deposits. The highland landforms (Cretaceous flysch and higher elevations of the Eocene flysch belts) are severely deformed by tectonic action and erosion, making many areas nearly impassable. Slopes on some of the higher plateaus are gentle enough to permit agriculture and long-distance communications. The rolling hills of the middle elevations (Eocene flysch belt beneath 200 m above sea level and the Neogene marine deposits) offer fine opportunities for agriculture and present fewer obstacles for transportation.

We must also consider climatic and cultural factors in combination with the dramatic nature of Sinop's physical topography if we seek to understand how people have perceived and inhabited this rich diverse environment.

The major factor that separates the ecology of the Pontic coast from the rest of Anatolia is the high rainfall (Figure 1-15). The prevailing winds from the north and west pick up moisture off the Black Sea and

Figure 1-14: The Akliman harbor from the southeast. The Karaada (Black island, also called Fener) on the north side of the fault is composed of Cretaceous volcanic bedrock, while the Sariada (Yellow island) on the south side of the fault is Plio-Quaternary sandstone.

dump it in the mountains. Rainfall distribution reflects local interactions between these two factors. The coast several hundred km west of Sinop is somewhat drier, the prevailing winds having picked up less moisture on a shorter pass over the sea; the eastern side toward Rize and Batumi is subtropical, with annual rainfall averaging over 2 m (Steinhauser 1970). Rainfall is distributed throughout the year, even in the summer months. The Sinop promontory projects out into this weather pattern. Its high mountains trap more rainfall on the western side above Ayancik, while the eastern side toward Gerze is somewhat drier. In Boyabat behind the coastal mountains the climate is much drier and continental, with hot summers and cold winters.

The diverse geological and climatic conditions of the Sinop promontory have also produced a rich and varied floral regime. In gen-

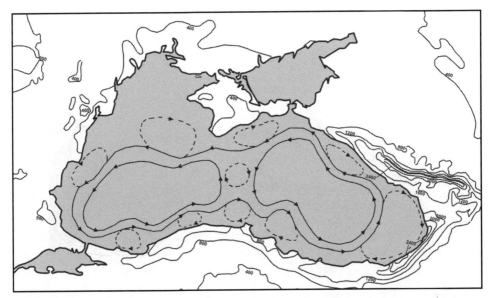

Figure 1-15: Climatic features of the Black Sea region including the primary and second-ary patterns of surface current circulation (continuous and dashed lines, respectively) and the annual rainfall in the Black Sea. The surface currents are strong enough to assist mariners crossing south to north from cape Carambis and from north to south from the Crimea to Sinop. Rainfall is measured in mm/year with isohyets at 400 mm intervals (based on data from Steinhauser 1970). Note the stark differences between the northern steppe and the southern and eastern mountain zones.

eral, Sinop belongs to the western side of the Euxine province of Turkey, drier than the sub-tropical regions east of Samsun (Davis 1965:5–6, 16–18; Sinop Valiligi 2002). The diverse ecology of the promontory is manifest in the composition of its forests, which varies with elevation and climate.

The coastal plains support a wide variety of broadleaf species, including many that bear edible fruit and nuts. The primary trees of the coast include oak, laurel, elm, plane, beech, boxwood, pine, hazelnut, chestnut, and cherry. As we move into the highlands, the forest compo-sitions start to become more distinct. In the lower elevations south of Ayancik the diverse forest regime includes fir, pine, beech, oak, plane, poplar, linden, and chestnut. At higher elevations the population thins almost exclusively to fir and scrub.

The forests behind Gerze are older and less diverse. Up to about 200 m above sea level diverse species include beech, boxwood, oak, pine, and

Figure 1-16: The forested highlands in Çakildak (near the location of Figure 1-10). Fir is the predominant species above 800 m.

fir. Between 200–800 m the forests are well developed with a tall canopy of beech and boxwood and a lower forest of mixed undergrowth. Wildflowers, smaller trees, and scrub quickly colonize areas opened up by fire or timber cutting. Above 800 m the forests are almost exclusively fir. These trees have been one of the great resources of Sinop since Classical times. The timber of Sinop has been singled out as among the best in the world for shipbuilding from the time of Theophrastus (ca. 400 BCE: *Enquiry into Plants* IV.5.5; Doonan 2002) to the 20th century (Tarkan 1941).

Traditional economic production in Sinop province reflects the same ecological diversity. The inland town of Boyabat just south of the Pontic mountains has a much drier climate (annual precipitation of 300–400 mm), and broad open plains that support all kinds of grain. The highlands behind Gerze and Ayancik have been the region's main sources of timber in Ottoman and Republican times.

The coastal lowlands have provided cash crops—in antiquity these areas were devoted to olive cultivation, in modern times tobacco. Fishing has been a staple of coastal production, although since 1985 the advent of large-scale capitalist fishing enterprises has disturbed traditional social balances and severely depleted fish stocks (Knudsen 1995). In the center of the promontory near the Eocene flysch/Plio-Quaternary marine transition (Erfelek) forest products including fruit and nuts earned limited cash (Tarkan 1941), but this area was essentially cut off from a cash economy until fairly recently.

Fresh vegetables grown in all parts of the province were not cash crops, but were produced primarily for local consumption. The wide variety of ecological contexts in Sinop promontory have tended to promote connection between complementary regions, but the intensity, organization, and nature of exchange have varied greatly depending on historical and cultural contexts.

The considerable diversity of the Sinop promontory should be clear by now. This volume is organized spatially as well as chronologically to highlight the nature of places at the nexus of cultural-historical and physical-ecological contexts. The next chapter discusses the methods we are using to study the hinterland, situating our methodology in the broader context of Mediterranean, Near Eastern, and Black Sea landscape studies. We will then embark on our exploration of the landscapes of the Sinop promontory, basing our chronological framework on the social and economic contexts of the hinterland that relate loosely to traditional historical periods. In each chronological horizon we will explore several different places of Sinop starting in the port and suburban landscapes of Boztepe. We shall then examine the Demirci valley on the coast about 15 km south of Sinop. The central and outer Karasu river valley running south-north through the center of the promontory from the highlands above Erfelek to the coast provides case studies of a second coastal valley and an inland fluvial plain. Discussion of Boztepe, the Demirci valley, and the central and outer Karasu valley are based on systematic archaeological surveys carried out from 1997 to 1999. Chaper 2 also presents the sampling and fieldwork programs. In post-colonial times we will also look at the highlands, although our investigations to date in this area have been limited to extensive survey, making proposals about life in these places very tentative.

I close this introductory chapter with a caution and a request. We are continuing to explore the landscapes discussed in this volume and anticipate doing so for some time to come. It is with that admission that we seek a measure of indulgence from the reader. This discussion, though based on evidence diligently recovered through the efforts of many, is itself a stage on a road to the fuller understanding of these land-scapes. Many of the hypotheses advanced here should be seen as works in progress rather than clearly demonstrated by authoritative fieldwork and documentary research. The final chapter will consider how far we have come and what further research we have to look forward to.

2

Landscape Archaeology in Sinop

The various processes that together comprised the Sinop promonto-ry's complex role in the Black Sea cannot be studied by excavating a single site, conducting a survey of a city's agricultural holdings, or assembling a body of relevant historical texts. Systems of communication, production, consumption, and identity production are situated in networks of places rather than in single places and so are best studied in a framework encompassing multiple places. Since 1990 multi-sited research designs have become more prominent in studies of complex cultural processes like globalization, diaspora formation, and trade (Appadurai 1990; Marcus 1995; Doonan 2001).

Of course, any archaeological landscape study is bound to be multi-sited, so how might such an approach be distinctive? Research topics like globalization, diaspora formation, and trade are situated in a network of locales and environments suited to analysis in multiple research arenas (Appadurai 1990; Bauer and Doonan 2002; Shami 2000). Rather than focusing on multiple places, multi-sited research follows the processes that connect distant physical and conceptual locations (Marcus 1995:105). These processes are the primary focus of multi-sited research rather than the patchwork of places that are connected by them. To these ends the Sinop fieldwalking program is designed to obtain information relevant to studying processes like exchange, warfare, production, consumption, and identity formation by sampling in locales connected by these processes (Doonan forthcoming). Each of these processes maps differently across many kinds of places in the landscapes and seascapes around Sinop.

The Sinop Regional Archaeological Project (SRAP) is the terrestrial component of the Black Sea Trade Project (BSTP), a program that investigates exchange, production, and culture formation around the Black Sea in terrestrial and maritime environments (Hiebert et al. 1997). BSTP and SRAP investigate diverse arenas in terms of environment (underwater, coastal, inland), time (Neolithic to early modern), and method. The integration of maritime and terrestrial arenas through exchange, production, warfare, and similar processes is a fundamental concept on which BSTP is based. The methods and preliminary results of the underwater research program are published elsewhere (Ballard et al. 2002) and will not be considered further here.

The sampling program on land gathers information on a wide array of environmental and topographical contexts that are connected through social and cultural processes. Diverse methods (remote sensing, surface survey, excavation, geomorphology, geophysics, materials analysis, historical-documentary research, and ethnography) and survey designs (transect sampling, quadrat sampling, and on-site evaluation) enable us to study the connections between places. It is equally important to gather data that can be compared to research projects in other areas, both those with specific cultural and historical connections (Mediterranean, Near Eastern, Steppe) and case studies of port-hinterland relationships in other parts of the world.

Space and Place: The Contexts of Human Action

We have already begun to explore the nature of places as intersections between physical-ecological settings and human interpretations. Landscapes might be considered to be sets or systems of places that are seen as belonging together by inhabitants, the people who operate within a landscape. The human interpretive processes that interpret meaningful sets of places are conditioned by cultural and historical factors, in addition to individual goals and interests. Thus a landscape is shifting and dynamic, not a static unit. Furthermore, an archaeological landscape is not the same as the many different landscapes that have overlapped with places and locales within it.

In a diverse region like that of Sinop promontory people inhabit different places in different ways. Inhabitants perceive meanings and potentials in places prompting many different responses. Historical or sacred associations might encourage marking a place with a monument or ritual that may or may not leave traces for archaeologists to detect later. These meanings and interpretations help to create ideational landscapes that people engage in different ways based on particular cultural and historical contexts (Knapp and Ashmore 1999).

From the early occupation of Sinop people have perceived and taken advantage of the diverse economic opportunities offered by the promontory. A wide range of social responses has allowed communities to live in these varied places: at some times complementary products have been exploited through mobile hunting-gathering, while at others local products have been shared among sedentary communities through exchange. Social control over landscapes might be asserted through the establishment of land tenure systems, the clarification of community boundaries, or the association of places with social strata such as elite vs. common. Relationships can be regulated or formalized through such political or religious institutions as colonies, temples, or ports.

Humans transform places and landscapes in ways that have profound effects on the nature and condition of the archaeological record. Forest clearance, agriculture, building, and other activities can obscure or highlight preexisting evidence at the same time that these activities themselves are also part of the topic we are studying. Those parts of Sinop promontory where we have sufficient visibility to study were mostly cleared for agriculture in Ottoman times (mid–15th–early–20th centuries). Deforestation has destabilized upland soils that have been redeposited in alluvial floodplains and deltas. Newly deposited soils cover earlier archaeological contexts. Plowing and planting has disturbed archaeological contexts but at the same time made them visible for surface survey. These examples show the complex effects that human activities (called c-transforms by Schiffer 1987) have on the archaeological record. Wandsnider (2001) refers to landscapes as archaeological palimpsests, collections of transformations that accrue over time, rather than making arbitrary boundaries between archaeological and "post-depositional" components of landscapes.

Recently archaeologists amenable to the post-processual paradigm have begun to emphasize the importance of studying human action in humanized places. This approach is different from the conventional view of landscape as a neutral space that humans respond to in a mechanical way (Tilley 1994; Bender 1998). Human action in landscapes depends on perception and interpretation, so in order to understand how humans interact with landscape means we must try to "walk in their shoes." Imagination, memory, and experience all contribute to a humanized view of a place and help to shape what we do there.

Considering landscapes from a humanized perspective prioritizes the human perceptions and interpretations of landscapes from phenomenological, social, and religious standpoints (Tilley 1994; Bradley 2000). Landscapes acquire meanings through experiences and interpretations built up over time. They are not abstract containers easily subjected to neutral descriptive analysis.

The highly visible places known to archaeologists as sites are places that have been transformed by repeated or intensive human action. Conventional sites can be the places where a house, temple, or bridge has stood, the dead have been buried, refuse has been deposited, intensive processing of materials has taken place, and so on. These are important places in the human experience of a landscape, but no more so than those places where animals were grazed, crops were grown, or about which a myth has been told (Dunnell 1992). Meanings are derived from perceived qualities in the landscape and inscribed by habitual action (Tilley 1994:15-30).

Tilley's critiques of positivist approaches to landscape have emphasized the imaginary and emotional responses of researchers to landscapes in evoking possible past experiences of places. While his critiques have been effective and influential, it is more difficult to realize many of his goals in fieldwork. Tilley's approach has been applied in his reconsideration of highly visible megalithic monuments in Britain and has now been brought into an active field program at Lesternick (Bender et al. 2001). These studies celebrate the subjective experiences of fieldworkers in a profusion of feelings, hunches, theories, brainwaves, and stories. However interesting these observations are, it is difficult to compare such results to those from other projects. SRAP has developed a multi-level approach to sampling that is designed to be sensitive to a humanized perspective but not so subjective that results cannot be compared to other regional projects in the Mediterranean and western Asia. The quadrat-based sampling program encourages team members to record and consider broader landscape contexts than individual survey tracts, while collecting quantified data on the distribution of lithic and ceramic evidence within each tract that can be compared to similarly collected data from other projects.

Human perceptions of places depend on memories, senses, and practices. Most archaeologists take a distinctly "top down" approach to studying landscape, adopting the analytical perspective of a spy satellite

Figure 2-1: Intensive fieldwalking in the Sinop hinterland. In an intensive survey design archaeologists walking in controlled paths spread at known intervals carefully scrutinize the soil for traces of human activity.

while gathering field data on foot. The information gathered on the ground is collected by fieldwalkers who are spread at known intervals (usually 10–20 m) who carefully scour the ground beneath their feet for traces of pottery, building materials, and other evidence that people have altered the place in some way (Figure 2-1). Intensive field survey is not the only way to approach a landscape. One can investigate a landscape in a more extensive mode, interpreting the surrounding landscape and reacting to features like roads, cleared forests, and built-up terraces that have been developing over millennia.

SRAP is integrating strategies encourage a heads-up approach to systematic survey. The quadrat-based sampling program samples units that are limited enough in spatial extent to be characterized as places in the sense discussed above. Quadrat sizes range from 0.5 to 2 km2 in area and can be characterized in terms of topography, vegetation, soil, and relationships to other places in the archaeological landscape. The scale of quadrats as sampling units encourages the interpretation of the broader patterns in a landscape as well as obtaining quantified data on the distribution of ceramic and lithic evidence in on-, near-, and off-site contexts.

Despite the rigorous standards of collection in a systematic field survey, field data are messy. They are gathered under highly variable field conditions, judged in the hot sun on the fly as to date and meaning, initially deposited by the chaotic processes through which humans deal with unwanted stuff, and transformed by a host of archaeological formation processes. The factors that determine the distribution of archaeological evidence include the human circumstances of its production, use, and deposition. For example a pot placed in a particular spot may have been imported or local, purchased or home made, used for food storage, consumption, or showing off, and may have in the end been abandoned, thrown out, or deliberately deposited somewhere as part of a ritual. The position of that pot may have changed when a farmer plowed the field or dug a pit, a road was cut, or the soil around the pot was dug up to be used as fill somewhere else. Schiffer (1987) has termed the various processes that create the archaeological record as we find it "formation processes." He calls those processes brought about by human action "C-transforms" and those that come about by natural action (erosion, tectonics, weathering) "N-transforms."

Good surveys take note of complicated formation processes and factors affecting field observations while doing fieldwork. But more often than not, field data have to be isolated from their complex contexts in order to impose analytical rigor. Finally the data are all marshaled on extensive tables and in charts showing densities per field and date in order to demonstrate particular models for economic and social behavior.

Recently Geographic Information Systems (GIS) have emerged as essential tools for organizing the array of information that is gathered in the course of fieldwork (for a good discussion of a recent example see Gillings and Sbonias 1999). GIS are databases that are organized spatially with layers of variables linked to sets of points or shapes. GIS databases allow any information that can be linked to the base map to be conveniently stored, retrieved, and analyzed statistically against other data sets. Despite the great potential of preserving more contextual information together with field data, eliminating subjectivity from our field data remains a problem. Rather than eliminating subjectivity from landscape studies it might be better to integrate interpretive observations about landscapes and the processes of gathering archaeological evidence with objective evidence (such as soil types, landform types, areas, and densities of archaeological evidence) in a controlled system that yields both comparable results and rich interpretations (Foss 2001).

Patchiness and Graininess in Human Landscapes

The utility of synthesizing regional-scale landscape data sets is indisputable, but we are attempting to foreground a smaller-scale perspective. Rather than following the traditional narrative structure proceeding from one period to the next in a totalizing history of a study area, we might consider historical processes in a way that highlights the importance of places. Do certain qualities of some places lead to persisting patterns of economic and social behavior? For example, did the easy waterborne transportation between Sinop port and the coast of the Demirci valley lead to the emergence of cash crops and manufacturing in Demirci during those periods (especially late Roman and late Ottoman) when the port and hinterland economies were strongly linked? In more general terms, how have human perceptions of the meanings and potentials of places led to recognizable patterns of action?

Human interpretations of landscape depend on perceived economic, ideational, and historical qualities. We inscribe meaning on landscapes through praxis—habitual action and interpretation (Knapp and Ashmore 1999). Landscapes are cultural structures like languages (Bourdieu 1977; Tilley 1994) and are created by such practices as agriculture, industry, travel, and religious worship. Each place is rich in an array of features that can prompt a wide range of responses from human inhabitants. A landscape that is perceived as relatively homogeneous might be used in a similar way across an extensive area. On the other hand, a landscape that is seen as diverse might have a wide range of complementary activities each concentrated in a limited space. The traditional pattern of transhumance along the Pontic coast of Turkey is a good example. Communities that spend winters in near-coastal villages take advantage of the rich fish resources and mild climate and in the summer remove to the rich arboreal fruits and lush pastures of the highland camps (*yaylas*). One of our challenges as archaeologists is to judge to what extent our investigations are sufficiently detailed and extensive to shed light on the range and structure of human activities in a given place.

The ecological concepts of patch, patchiness, and grain provide useful analogies for modeling the potentials for social and economic processes in different inhabited landscapes (Winterhalder 1994). Patches are local discontinuities in a landscape with distinctive properties that affect the behavior of particular organisms and processes. Patchiness is the degree to which patches are widely or unevenly dispersed through a landscape (Winterhalder 1994:33). In an ecosystem graininess is a measure of the scale of patchiness relative to the typical range of a given organism. In a cultural context graininess might balance the scale of economic production or commodity consumption against the distribution of landscape and cultural features perceived as advantageous for carrying out those activities.

Patches in a human economic landscape might be based on the distribution of certain soil types, topographic conditions, raw materials, and such social factors as access to communications or potential for specialized production in a complex regional economy. The lower elevations (up to ca. 200 masl) of the Sinop promontory are relatively fine grained with evenly dispersed resources from the standpoint of agricultural production. However, from the standpoint of long-range or high-volume transport the coasts are at a distinct advantage over the interior, the high ridges over the foothills, and so on (Figure 2-2). Ridges within view of the sea were seen as good places for tumulus cemeteries in Hellenistic times (for example, see Demirci and Akliman quadrats in Chapter 4) while different local economic conditions led to the widespread settlement of the former and the near abandonment of the latter in Roman times.

Patchiness is an important factor to keep in mind when establishing and evaluating a sampling design. Sampling is a critical element of modern archaeological research (Orton 2000). Probabilistic sampling, the extrapolation of patterns from the intensive study of randomly selected sample zones, has been one of the central theoretical principles of surface survey in the Mediterranean since the late 1970s (Cherry 1982; Wright et al. 1991; Orton 2000). Sampling in systematic archaeological survey is the examination of study areas by walking over them with a team of field walkers spread out at known intervals. Low resolution sampling would spread field walkers out widely in order to cover large areas in a short amount of time. High-resolution sampling would keep field walkers close together making it likely that small discontinuities in the distribution of material evidence could be observed. In developing a strategy to study a particular landscape we must attune our fieldwork to

Figure 2-2: A highland road follows a ridge west of Gerze.

the different kinds of evidence bearing on different kinds of economic and ideational potentials. A low-resolution sampling program might cover a lot of ground but miss small-scale or less visible evidence. A high-resolution but spatially limited program might not be sufficiently extensive to detect meaningful relationships between several sets of settlements together with their productive, agricultural and marginal territories (Wandsnider 1998).

Archaeologists studying people and landscapes need to develop sampling programs that are sensitive to the ways people have inhabited landscapes. In 1990, Fish and Kowalewski made a strong case for the usefulness of full-coverage survey that has had a powerful impact on research in the Mediterranean region. They argued that the chances of misinterpreting a landscape because a critical site was missed during a strict sampling program were too great. Full coverage of survey areas offered the most easily standardized sample and reduced the chances that critical sites would not be missed. Full coverage does not imply surveying everything, but it aims for an extensive sample with as few gaps as possible

(Cowgill 1990). But even an extensive contiguous survey is a sample. If a region were defined as the size of the Sinop promontory (25 x 25 km) the intensity of coverage would have to be so low that most small archaeological features would be missed. On the other hand, if the size of the survey area were small enough to sample at a high resolution it would be too limited to address larger-scale problems like the organization of inter-settlement communication systems, trade, and production.

On the other hand a multi-site study of an extensive area like the Sinop promontory does not allow full coverage. In this case a combination of surveys at different levels of resolution can be an effective way to conduct research in a complex archaeological landscape with diverse cultural phases and low visibility (Plog 1990).

Returning to the concept of patches, one way to develop a sampling program sensitive to various multi-sited processes and cultural contexts would be to distribute sample areas so that they cover patches significant in particular cultural contexts at appropriate levels of resolution. For example, our research to date suggests that most Bronze Age settlements are between 10 and 20 m across. Bronze Age pottery scatters are not smeared across the landscape by plowing in contrast to Hellenistic and Roman settlements that can have extensive scatters of displaced pottery beyond the primary settlement area. Bronze Age settlements have seldom been observed to date separated by less than 1 km. A sampling program that would document Bronze Age settlement would need to position field walkers close enough together to detect clusters of lithics and pottery 10 m across, and to work in sampling units sufficiently extensive to reasonably test for presence/ absence of features at a density of about 1 per km2. If sample areas of 0.5 km2 were chosen then several samples would need to be centered on each patch type being investigated (for instance coastal beach, coastal ridge, near-coastal slope, inland terrace, and so on). As with any sampling program the results are not foolproof, but at least we should be able to gauge where evidence is likely to be insufficient to make reliable generalizations.

After estimating the scales and densities at which certain activities were carried out we can proceed to ask what is the likelihood that such activities might be missed given the sample that has been obtained (Wandsnider 1998)? This strategy should prove more helpful than relying on a standard sampling fraction when assessing whether a survey has collected sufficient data to answer particular questions, because it takes into account critical factors that are specific to the particular objectives and cultural contexts.

Given the kinds of questions a project is trying to answer, are the data collected sufficient to answer core questions? If not, what should the next steps be? To date SPRS has been more concerned with documenting the production, consumption, and circulation of goods through the promontory than in drawing up models for Bronze Age nearest neighbor analysis or documentation of debris scatters around Ottoman settlements. As such questions come to the foreground we will assess the weaknesses in our data to that point and develop sampling programs to address those questions. This approach is in essence applying the logic of the Bayesian school of statistics to archaeological and cultural questions (Buck et al. 1996; Orton 2000). Similarly, we would do well to look at how we can build upon the diverse kinds of information already available in order to refine our subsequent sampling. We will consider these questions in greater detail in Chapter 7.

Landscape Archaeology in the Mediterranean, Near East, and Black Sea

Landscape archaeology is one of the fastest developing paths we have toward understanding the past (Kardulias 1994b). The pace of development in systematic archaeological field survey in the Mediterranean has been breathtaking since the mid–1980s. The rapid advances in GIS and Global Positioning Systems (GPS) have accompanied a welcome trend toward longer-term multi-disciplinary regional studies. These developments have brought some research programs to the verge of achieving full-coverage surveys of regions, for example the Boeotia survey (Bintliff and Snodgrass 1985; Bintliff et al. 1999) and the Keos survey (Cherry et al. 1991).

Systematic Mediterranean surveys have proved particularly effective in establishing patterns of economic production and demography for the pottery-rich Greek and Roman times. Equally important has been a trend away from site-focused archaeology and toward understanding landscapes in more holistic terms. Highly intensive surveys with field-walkers spaced 10 m apart have been able to document ever smaller and subtler traces of human activity.

Surveys in the Near East have followed a somewhat different tradition (Wilkinson 2000). The strong emphasis on geographic modelling of relative site sizes and distributions encouraged many researchers to conduct low-intensity full-coverage surveys (Sumner 1990), while others relied on sampling-based methods (Adams 1981). In Mesopotamia the relatively good visibility in places unaffected by alluvial deposits combined with the highly visible tells (stratified mounds sticking up from the plain) characteristic of many periods has encouraged extensive field methods that severely underestimate small flat sites (Wilkinson 2000). However, these shortcomings are compensated for in part by the extensive geographic scale at which demographic and political organization can be studied (Adams 1981; Wilkinson 2000).

Alcock's (1993) seminal study of the landscapes of Roman Greece was a remarkable synthesis of information from archaeological surveys, imposing imperial monuments, and literary statements by Greeks, Romans, and post-antique visitors. Her comparative study of survey projects in Greece established levels of confidence in different styles of field survey based on the kinds of data that were collected and methods employed (Alcock 1993:33-37). Her ranking of surveys into (A) intensive-systematic, (B) intensive with limited sampling and (C) extensive-unsystematic was necessary in order to establish the ways in which data from dozens of projects might be considered together. Although she went on to use information from all types of projects usefully, her ranking of survey types has been heralded as a clear call for systematic-intensive survey as the most legitimate means of exploring landscapes.

Successful projects like the Keos survey (Cherry et al. 1991), the Pylos Regional Archaeological Project (Davis 1998), and the Leptiminus survey (Mattingly et al. 1995) have led to a strong emphasis on intensive systematic survey in the Mediterranean. This style of survey is very effective for answering questions about the nature of economic production or land tenure in parts of the Mediterranean where there is little vegetation and where limited post-antique soil development make archaeological evidence easy to see (Cherry 1994). However, such approaches are less effective in environments where abundant plant growth or significant post-antique soil development severely hamper archaeological visibility. The Sinop promontory— more than 54% forested, over 500 km2 in extent, and bewildering in its ecological and cultural diversity—seemed to offer little opportunity for the kind of survey that has been so successful in the Mediterranean. When the questions we were asking about multi-sited processes were added to the picture, meaning that it was necessary to develop a perspective covering much of the promontory, the prospects of conducting research that could be compared to Mediterranean surveys appeared daunting indeed.

Extensive Survey

In order to overcome the challenges of extensive survey in a region with dense vegetation and heavy forestation we are developing a field program consisting of investigations at different spatial scales (transects, ca. 5–10 km2, quadrats, ca. 1–2 km2, settlements), intensities (extensive, intensive), and methods (surface survey, geophysics, geomorphology, small excavations). We began with an extensive survey in 1996. An extensive survey explores a large territory with a comparatively low intensity of coverage. This type of survey makes use of information provided by local inhabitants and previous visitors in order to develop a sense of how the form and setting of the largest and most obvious loci (places where evidence of human occupation, worship, burial, industry, or other activity is observed).

Extensive surveys are good for finding a great number of large or otherwise highly visible sites that attract much attention from local inhabitants. They encourage archaeologists to approach landscapes more like the way inhabitants do: interpreting historical, ecological, and topographic features as they come into view. Despite the advantages of extensive surveys for documenting the most prominent archaeological features over a wide area, by themselves they are less effective for rigorously documenting social and economic behavior.

The extensive survey allowed us to develop preliminary ideas about how the landscapes of Sinop might be approached and to assess what kinds of conditions and landforms had to be taken into consideration. In Sinop we divided the promontory into different topographic and environmental zones to be sampled (Figure 2-3). Zones were defined based on predominant physical and geographical properties that we thought might create different sets of patches. Ecological and physical properties include physical topography, bedrock and soil types, rainfall, and plant cover. Cultural-historical properties of these zones included factors influencing communications (relationships to the main port, coasts, and potential and known communications routes), mineral and other resources, and presence of natural features that were often perceived by Black Sea and Mediterranean cultures as sacred (mountaintops, caves, and other prominent formations).

We use the term "locus" (plural loci) to refer to a place where evidence has been documented for human activity before the 20th century. Locus is a more effective term than the more commonly used "site" because that term has become associated with a style of landscape

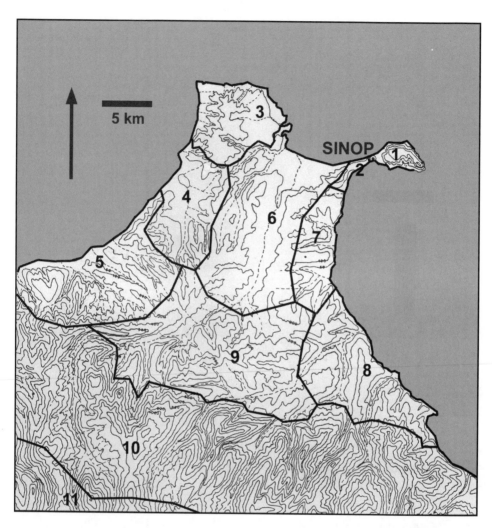

Figure 2-3: Environmental and topographic zones on the Sinop promontory. Each zone was sampled in the extensive survey of the promontory. Zones were defined based on their ecological and physical properties, their relationship to the port, coasts, potential communications routes, and cultural-historical and environmental factors. (1) Boztepe, (2) Sinop near hinterland, (3) Inceburun, (4) west coast valleys (outer promontory), (5) west coast (rough to Ayancik), (6) Karasu valley, (7) east coast valleys (outer promontory), (8) east coast (rough near Gerze), (9) middle highlands near Erfelek, (10) highlands, (11) Kizilirmak-Gökirmak valley.

archaeology that prioritizes only the hot spots rich in artifacts rather than trying to understand human interactions with and in landscapes (Dunnell 1992).

Extensive investigations of Sinop promontory helped us to understand some basic factors that were valuable in designing our systematic surveys. Each of these factors varied considerably in different zones and over the cultural and historical phases of human life on the promontory. How big were settlements, industrial areas, and agricultural fields in various kinds of places? How extensive were the emptier spaces that separated loci of various kinds? Were edges and centers of intensive human activity marked by symbolically rich features like temples, shrines, cemeteries, and markets?

When we consider landscapes that were inhabited by more than one cultural-historical community we must keep in mind that each group may have responded differently to evolving landscapes. Responses to landscapes depended on the size of a community and the nature of its economic and social activities. In an archaeological landscape we might be tracing prehistoric encampments, Roman suburban industry, and a dispersed Ottoman village. Certain features like settlement mounds, city walls, and road systems clearly influenced subsequent use.

Archaeologically detectable activities of the various people who have inhabited an archaeological landscape would have been distributed differently and at many different spatial scales. When an archaeologist stands in a particular location, that place may in the past have been a part of Bronze Age, then Roman and Ottoman landscapes. It is difficult to study these landscapes together, as one of the leading archaeological survey teams in Greece has lamented (Bintliff 1999). A survey that documents a Greco-Roman industrial landscape effectively may not be as good at analyzing dispersed prehistoric villages. This is why we have undertaken several different strategies in walking the landscapes of Sinop.

Systematic Survey

From 1997 to 1999 we conducted systematic-intensive surveys in the Demirci and Karasu valleys and the southern slopes of Boztepe (Figure 2-4). In each of these we prioritized high-visibility conditions, sampling fewer km2 than surveys striving toward full coverage and collecting rich field data on the distribution of ceramic ware types and shapes. We sampled lower-visibility areas using more extensive techniques and made use

Figure 2-4: CORONA photograph of the Sinop promontory highlighting the Boztepe, Demirci, and Karasu valley sample quadrats. Dark areas are heavily forested, offering almost no potential for systematic archaeological survey.

of information from local people to contextualize the results from intensive survey. Results obtained from opportunistic investigations were not tallied together with data from systematic work. The information gathered in the Karasu and Demirci valleys belongs partly to our systematic survey and partly to our extensive survey data sets, since loci identified on the basis of interviews with local inhabitants could not be tallied together with the systematic data set. A short introduction to each of these three survey areas will help place us in the archaeological landscapes.

Boztepe

We began to explore the headland of Boztepe (ancient Skopelos Mons) at the beginning of Chapter 1. This impressive (approximately 3 x 5 km)

volcanic mass looms 200 m above the sea. The defensibility and fertility of the headland were praised by Strabo in the 1st century BCE
(*Geography* XII.iii.15) and later authors. Precipitous cliffs dominate the
north and east coasts, while erosion has carved somewhat easier landings
along the south coast. The west slopes more gently down to a sandy
bridge that connects Boztepe to the mainland. The top of the promontory was flattened out for a modern military base by bulldozing soil off
the north and west slopes. Springs run down from the flat limestone formations at the top of the volcanic mass, where a small lake (Sulluk gölü)
formed.

Two harbors shelter boats on the north and south sides of Boztepe.
Of these the far more important is the southern, which is the best deepwater harbor on the south coast of the Black Sea. The isthmus has been
occupied by the town of Sinop since the 7th century BCE. Later on the
suburbs and city spread up the west slopes of Boztepe. Since the mid-
twentieth century the upper slopes have been dominated by a NATO
radar installation. Nearly everywhere on the north coast is either precip-
itously steep or under military restriction. The south slopes are relatively open for investigation, so we concentrated on these for the Boztepe
survey.

The south slopes of Boztepe have been farmed intermittently since
antiquity. Limited colluvial deposits have collected on the valley floors,
but erosional processes have not obscured much of this quadrat. The
survey spot checked valley floors that show evidence of erosion or heavy
vegetation that would obscure archaeological remains. A much wider
area is under threat by intensive ongoing development that destroys evidence of settlement and land use through excavation and displacement
of soils (see Figure 4-7 below).

Demirci Valley

The Demirci valley opens onto the east-facing shoreline of the Sinop
promontory about 15 km south of Sinop port. The valley is defined on
its north side by a ridge (maximum elevation about 150 m, see Eldevuz
and Demirci quadrats) running about 5 km inland from the coast. The
western watershed is defined by the ridge that runs south-north along
the eastern flank of the Karasu river (Uzungurgen N and S quadrats).
The southern side of the valley is more broken up, defined by a range of
low hills and side valleys oriented southwest-northeast. The Keçioglu
ridge runs along the shore on the south side of the valley, pinching

together with the Demirci ridge to constrict the seaward exit of the valley.

Soils on the slopes are composed of recently weathered mixed marine bedrock, washing down onto the valley floor. Some soil formation has been observed on the ridge where the forest covered some of the Roman agricultural fields. These forests were probably cleared in later Ottoman times during the expansion of hinterland settlement. The colluvial soils along the coast are particularly unstable on top of clay beds, which were used for the Roman ceramic industry here. SRAP has avoided systematic sampling on the valley floor where late antique and modern colluvial deposits have obscured earlier surfaces.

Sightlines connect most of the Demirci valley to the sea and coastal areas are visibly connected to the port of Sinop. The sea is visible from the north ridge (Demirci and Eldevuz quadrats) and terraces of the inner valley (Uzungurgen N and S quadrats). Boztepe is easily visible from the shore (Keçioglu quadrat). These sightlines may help to explain the valley's longstanding close ties to the port and its integration into the Black Sea economy in most periods after the establishment of the port of Sinope.

Karasu Valley

The melting snows and heavy rains of spring rush down from the narrow gorges of the Eocene flysch highlands in the upper Karasu river valley (ca. 1,300 m above sea level), but the stream slows to a trickle by late summer. As the river flows down into the Plio-Quaternary marly sandstone of the lower promontory the Karasu valley broadens into an open plain. The erratic violence of the spring flood has cleared out the floodplain regularly, creating an open landscape overlooked by terraces that have been occupied persistently since the Early Bronze Age. Our research in the central Karasu valley has focused on the terraces above the floodplain on the east bank of the river (Hacioglu and Nohutluk quadrats).

From about 4 km inland to the present coast the river and runoff from side valleys have been filling in a delta from the early Holocene onward (see Figure 1-11; Besonen in Doonan et al. 2001). Much of the Karasu delta was marshy and impassable in antiquity, and the valley floor up to about the 10 m contour is covered in colluvial fills (Besonen in Doonan et al. 2001). Our research in the delta area focused on the coast (Akliman, Bostancili quadrats) and the ridges overlooking the val-

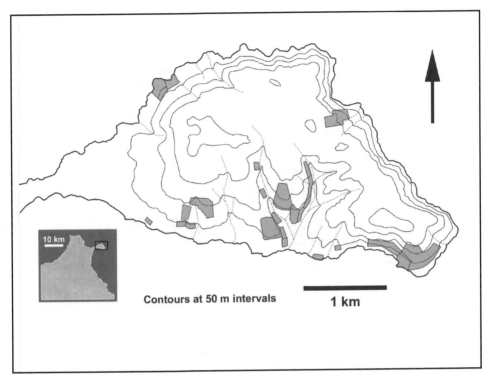

Figure 2-5: Surveyed tracts on Boztepe. A survey quadrat overlooking the south coast consisted of 21 tracts.

ley floor from the south (Osmaniye quadrat) and west (Dibekli, Sarsi quadrats).

Quadrat Surveys

Our systematic survey adopts three main field research strategies, each designed to collect different kinds of information. The surveys on Boztepe (Figure 2-5) and in the Demirci (Figure 2-6) and Karasu (Figures 2-7, 2-8) valleys thus far have been based on irregular polygonal units called quadrats. Each quadrat is a sample area about 1–2 km2 in extent in which we sample the plowed and planted agricultural fields that offer good visibility. About 10–25% of the fields in each quadrat are examined by teams of fieldwalkers each spread 10 m apart who collect information about the ceramics and other evidence visible around them. The units that each fieldwalker analyzes are called field transects, not to

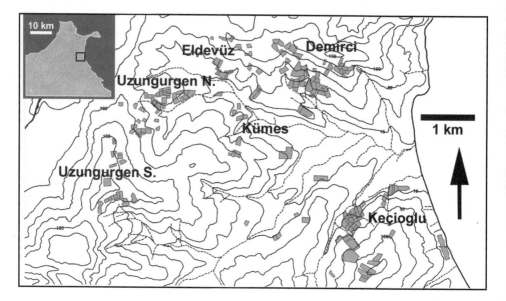

Figure 2-6: Surveyed tracts in the Demirci valley where six survey quadrats were sampled (west-east): (1) Uzungurgen S, (2) Uzungurgen N, (3) Eldevüz, (4) Kümes, (5) Demirci, (6) Keçioglu

be confused with the sample transects (larger sampling units discussed below) (Figure 2-9).

The nature of the data we collected was expanded from the Demirci valley (1997) survey to the Karasu valley survey (1998–1999). In 1997 fieldwalkers recorded field transects on the 1:25,000 topographic maps provided by the Turkish government. Observations were noted about discernible scatters of ceramics, roof tiles, and other evidence. Scatters were measured and sketched, but quantitative data on ceramic density were not collected. Quantitative information about ceramic density was also not collected as part of the Boztepe survey owing to the variable conditions of the fields we sampled. In 1998 we began to use digital cameras to document full ceramic assemblages from each field transect walked (Figure 2-10). Fieldwalkers picked up 100% of the ceramics observed in 1-m field transects for recording. After counting, weighing, photographing, and collecting information about different ceramic ware types almost all of the ceramics collected were left in the field.

Distinctive ware types and diagnostic sherds were kept for further study at the Sinop Regional Museum. Members of the team are establishing a ware-based typology of local ceramics in collaboration with the

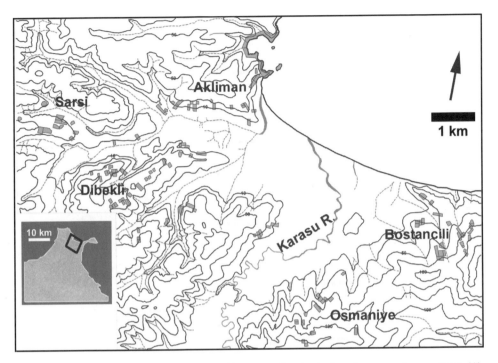

Figure 2-7: Surveyed tracts in the outer Karasu valley including five sample quadrats: (1) Akliman, (2) Bostancili, (3) Sarsi, (4) Dibekli, (5) Osmaniye.

Smithsonian Center for Materials Research and Education (Bauer in preparation). By keying this typology directly into ceramics document-ed in the field we are establishing a basis for meaningful quantitative studies of the distribution of ceramics and related commodities in a region where the ceramic assemblages are still poorly understood.

The location of quadrats was determined by our interest in survey-ing diverse patches, as suggested by topography, ecology, and cultural-historical factors. In the Demirci and Karasu valleys we surveyed 14 quadrats in over 300 survey tracts (Figures 2-7 to 2-9). In each valley quadrats were walked near the coasts, in areas accessible to but not on the coasts (1–3 km from the coast), along low-lying inland terraces, at the edges of river floodplains and watersheds. On Boztepe the large mil-itary base and extensive disruptions caused by modern building limited our effective sample to the slopes facing the south harbor (Figure 2-4).

The concept of patches, those features and concentrations of criti-cal resources that affect decision making about the use of places in land-scapes, is critical to the development of our quadrat sampling program.

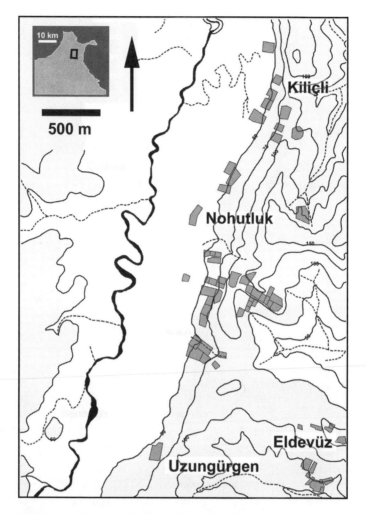

Figure 2-8: Surveyed tracts in the central Karasu valley including two sample quadrats: (1) Kiliçli, (2) Hacioglu.

Each quadrat offers a detailed look at a sample including various loci and off-site areas. Each quadrat is a place on a scale that inhabitants could easily look over or cross on foot in an hour. Formal field transects are only walked in tracts that have been recently plowed and offer good visibility in order to maintain comparability from tract to tract and quadrat to quadrat. Notes are taken on topography and resources around each tract, and a sketch map of observations in the tract is prepared as a key to the information about finds described above.

Figure 2-9: The central Karasu valley as seen from the north.

Assessing how much sampling is necessary to constitute an effective sample depends on the graininess of the landscapes we are studying. Graininess depends on range, which in the case of human-settlement systems is related to the scale and intensity of cultural activities, the likely density of those activities, and the relationship of particular activities to particular resources and features.

People in Bronze Age, Roman, and Ottoman cultural contexts inhabited the Sinop promontory landscapes differently, affecting the graininess of landscapes. Although our information is still too limited to make confident interpretations, some working hypotheses may be advanced. Most Bronze Age settlements, such as Kocagöz in the Demirci valley, were small and self-sufficient, situated to take advantage of a diverse terrestrial resource base. It appears in the later Bronze Age and Iron Age that coastal locations, such as Akliman, Sinop Kale NW, and Gerze-Kösk höyük, were favored for settlement (for location see Figure

Figure 2-10: Ceramics from a field transect in the Karasu valley. Digital photographs like this were taken of ceramics from every field transect in the Karasu survey to allow us to study the distribution of wares from tract to tract and quadrat to quadrat.

3-1). This may reflect a more specialized economy, including a maritime component (perhaps fishing or exchange).

Precolonial settlements were widely dispersed and compact, with broad interstitial spaces. Reliable estimation of the presence or absence of precolonial settlements requires extensive coverage of continuous areas, which in Sinop means that we must work in places with both good and poor visibility. One of the deficiencies of our quadrat sampling program to date is that extensive systematic coverage of places with poor visibility has not yet been carried out.

On the other hand, several Roman (2nd-7th century CE) settlements and industrial facilities such as Uzungurgen N and Karapinar were set on terraces and ridges overlooking valleys that offered potential for extensive agriculture (for the locations of Roman loci see Figure 5-1). Settlements that appear to have had a specialized coastal function were also observed from Roman times. Some, like Gerna, were probably responding to economic opportunities (fishing, coastal way station) made possible by the highly integrated Roman economy. Others like the suburban structure (possibly a villa) at Kiraztepe revealed the development and spread of suburban elite settlements. Roman settlement tended to be extensive, specialized, and connected. One of the problems the quadrat survey seeks to address is the movement of goods between distinctive patches in the Roman landscape. Because of the specialized nature of Roman exploitation, the different resources and topographic features in the landscape conditioned decisions about use more strongly consistent with a coarse grain (that is a landscape offering diverse potentials).

The Sinop promontory can be seen as fine grained in precolonial times with extensive low-density settlement distribution. In Roman and late Ottoman–Republican times (19th–early 20th century) we note coarser graininess with extensive settlement. Early-middle Ottoman (15th–18th centuries) settlement patterns appear closer to the precolonial than the Roman, and so might suggest a more independent economic base despite the imperial social-political context (see Chapter 6). Difficulties in obtaining comparable records of Ottoman and Greco-Roman landscapes (Cherry 1994:102) may be resolved using complex sampling programs like those discussed above that are sensitive to diverse scales and density of settlement and production.

Locus-Scale Research

One of the critical challenges we face in surface-oriented archaeology is the interpretation of what the loci we find on the surface actually represent (van Andel and Runnels 1987; Murray and Kardulias 1988; Alcock 1994; Jameson 1995). Close investigations of individual loci can help us sort out some of the activities that people engaged in there in the past. Interpretation is not straightforward, since archaeological loci are merely the surface expression of a shifting history of activities (van Andel and Runnels 1987). For example, the coastal (plaj) settlement of Demirci plaj was first a settlement in a relatively local economy, it was then colonized as Greek-related settlements were established along this coast. It became a major ceramic production site followed by olive oil production in Roman times. It was abandoned in later Byzantine times and resettled as an Ottoman agricultural field. Finally in the later 20th century a

Table 2-1: Interpretations of Site Types Based on Surface Finds

Type	Extent	Material "Signature"
Settlement, Farm	< 1 ha	Mixed ceramics, construction debris (daub, tiles, mortar), clustering of storage-related and consumption-related ceramics
Settlement, Farm (outbuilding)	< 0.1 ha	Construction debris (roof tiles, stones), little pottery, soil discoloration
Settlement, Village/Hamlet	ca. 1–5 ha	Mixed ceramics, construction debris (daub, tiles, mortar), clustered distribution of material indicating different functions, multiple units suggested by clustering
Settlement, Town	5.0+ ha	Mixed ceramics, construction debris (daub, tiles, mortar), clustered distribution of material indicating differential functions, multiple units suggested by clustering
Cemetery	Various	Special finds in situ (sarcophagi, stelae), tumuli, human bones, fine pottery mixed with personal items, evidence of tumuli, cist tombs, and tile-lined tombs
Religious	Various	Fine or miniature ceramics, topographic features (springs, caves, mountain tops, outcrops), figurines, church-related architectural features
Ceramic Kilns	< 0.1 ha	Ceramic wasters, vitrified kiln bricks, soil discoloration

modern glass factory was established here. Each of these phases of inhabitation transformed the surface expressions of previous activities.

We employ a variety of techniques to interpret the loci we find in surface survey, including intensive collection of ceramics and other materials from the surface, and geomagnetic and other subsurface remote sensing techniques (Doonan et al. 2000). We are developing ways to use methods like geochemical sampling to establish areas where animals were kept, refuse deposited, and manuring of fields practiced around the ceramic scatters identified as loci. Excavations are planned at several key loci that show sufficient functional and chronological complexity to warrant them. But most loci must be interpreted solely on the basis of the distribution and nature of the material finds from the surface (Table 2-1).

Sample-Transect Surveys

We are supplementing the quadrat- and site-based investigations with surveys of long continuous transects that examine complex landscapes ranging from the coasts to the highlands in several different environmental and historical settings. By cutting across river valleys, coastal plains, upland ravines, and highland plateaus each transect will help us to understand the complexity of the different patches distributed through the Sinop terrain. Gathering data from contiguous tracts in larger units will improve our understanding of spatial relationships between loci and help to define more precisely cycles of settlement nucleation and dispersal. The sample transects also yield data sets that can be compared more directly with other Mediterranean and Near Eastern surveys.

Transects, including the east and west coasts of the promontory, will allow us to study the distinct cultural and ecological patches of the two sides of the promontory. Transects incorporating already-surveyed quadrats in the Karasu and Demirci valleys will help us to understand how patterns observed in the quadrat-based survey correspond to patterns in the extensive transect-surveys.

SRAP is building on existing approaches by suggesting that surveys in regions with complex settlement histories adopt diverse sampling programs that are adapted to be sensitive to the multiple landscapes we seek to understand. Despite the need to achieve consistent standards of recording, landscape coverage, and methods, each project needs to chart a course among goals, histories, and multiple landscapes (Mattingly 2000; Foss 2001; Wandsnider 2001).

3

Sinop before Colonial Times

People have lived in the Sinop promontory for 10,000 years or more, since before the Black Sea had even come to its present form, possibly in the 6th millennium BCE (Ryan et al. 1997; Hiebert 2001). The diversity of archaeological evidence in different parts of Sinop promontory suggests that the early cultures and economies of the promontory were as diverse as in later times. However, we will consider the cultural horizons before the expansion of Hellenistic settlement (3rd century BCE and later) together for two main reasons. First, the rudimentary state of the relative ceramic chronology defies sufficiently close discrimination to confidently assess the cultural context of certain hand-made ware types. Second, the quadrat sampling program has yielded an uneven picture of the small-scale settlements of these periods, sited for the most part on land marginal to modern farmers and so difficult to sample because of poor visibility.

Up until the later centuries of the 2nd or the beginning of the 1st millennium BCE people living in Sinop took advantage of the rich plant and animal resources available on land, with occasional forays on water. The places where people lived reflected their priorities: inland valleys and ridges and sites within view of the sea but not directly on the shore were frequently chosen from the Neolithic through much of the Bronze Age (ca. 6000–1000 BCE).

About the turn of the 1st millennium a new pattern appears to have emerged, with settlements forming directly on the coast (Figure 3-1). At

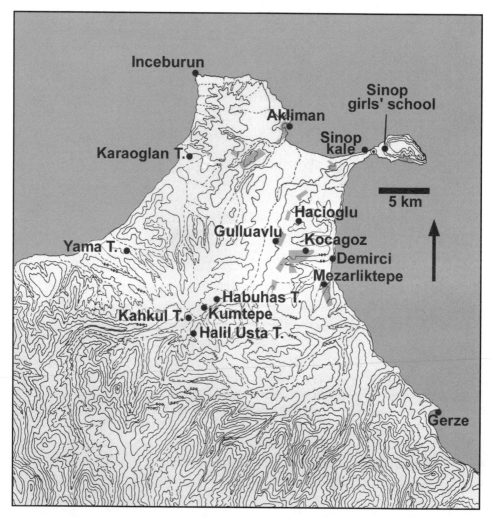

Figure 3-1: Precolonial sites on Sinop promontory.

times the ceramics and architecture of these settlements demonstrated close cultural connections to other parts of the Black Sea. Although it is tempting to see trade as an important component of the early Black Sea maritime economy, it is more likely that the early coastal sites took greater advantage of the rich cyclical migrations of fish passing by Sinop each year. During the 7th century BCE Greek colonists set up an outpost at Sinop port, orienting their economy almost exclusively toward maritime trade.

Figure 3-2: Chert scraper and blade from Inceburun.

The earliest traces of human habitation in the Sinop promontory have been recorded at the Inceburun headland, the northernmost point in Anatolia (Figure 1-13). The sparse scatter of late Upper Paleolithic (ca. 15000–10000 BC) chipped stone blades and other lithics from this locus (Figure 3-2) raise the possibility that the promontory was inhabited at the time when Ryan and Pittman have proposed the Black Sea was inundated (ca. 5700 BCE—Ryan et al. 1997).

New objections to the thesis of a catastrophic inundation of the Black Sea have recently been raised by researchers citing evidence of an open connection between the Sea of Marmara and the Black Sea over the past 10,000 years (Aksu et al. 2002). Regardless of whether Ryan and Pittman's proposed date and explanation of the filling of the Black Sea are correct, the Black Sea level was lower than it is today at the beginning of the Holocene, implying that Inceburun would have been inland at the time it was initially occupied (Hiebert 2001). Other parts of the promontory may have been occupied at this time, but the subsequent inundation and burial under up to 10 m of soil has frustrated attempts to document traces of this early period.

The transition from the earliest settlements to later prehistoric periods is unclear, but some settlements may have appeared by as early as the 6th millennium BCE. Ceramics showing parallels to 6th millennium settlements near the Sea of Marmara have been documented at the site of Mezarliktepe near the coast in the Demirci valley (Doonan and Gantos in preparation a). The dating of prehistoric ceramics in Sinop is problematic because of the lack of stratified settlements excavated to date. There is a tradition of assigning dates to the handmade ceramics from the area, but these typologies are not grounded by any chronometric or even relative stratified sequences. SRAP is undertaking a series of investigations clarifying the chronology of the hand-made ceramics, but for the purposes of this volume it is safer to err on the side of caution rather than to base elaborate models on unfounded chronology. Working hypotheses will be proposed here about some remains that show parallels with examples from better-dated excavations in other regions. However, without the underpinning of a well-founded local chronology we should not attempt to over-interpret a tenuous body of evidence.

Excavations at Ikiztepe, a major settlement about 90 km east of Sinop in the Kizilirmak river delta, define the chronology of central Pontic Anatolian pottery during the Chalcolithic (late 5th–4th millennium BCE) and Early Bronze Ages (3rd–early 2nd millennium BCE) periods (Alkim et al. 1988; Bilgi forthcoming). Ceramics from many places in the Sinop region can be compared to examples from Ikiztepe. The potters of the Kizilirmak delta worked under much stronger central Anatolian influence than their counterparts on the Sinop promontory. On the other hand, the Sinop region has shown greater receptivity to west and north Pontic influence, and so a greater dynamism might be expected in times when maritime interaction was more intensive (Hiebert 2001; Bauer forthcoming).

The inhabitants of the Chalcolithic and Early Bronze Ages settled in dispersed locations, particularly in places that offered a rich terrestrial catchment area. Although our information is still scant, people of the Early Bronze Age frequently chose to settle at prominent sites that looked on the sea or commanded open inland valleys. Some settlements like Yamatepe and Kocagöz, although not situated directly on the coast, were located close enough to the sea to offer some potential to exploit maritime resources. Ceramics from a few loci (e.g., Gulluavlu) suggest sporadic contacts with other parts of the Black Sea, particularly the north and west coasts (Bauer 2001; Doonan et al. 2001).

The Middle Bronze Age (first half of the 2nd millennium BCE) is difficult to trace, but a few loci suggest some contact with central Anatolia. Spouted and red-burnished wares reminiscent of contemporary sites in central Anatolia appear at a few loci in the Karasu valley and on the coast (Gulluavlu, Kösk Höyük, Gerze: see Isin 1998:pl. 10). This pattern may be understood in the context of preliminary results from the highlands above the Karasu and Kabali rivers. The prehistoric ceramic technologies in this area show an unusual degree of coherence that may suggest cooperation and communication. The distinctive red lime-tempered wares of these highlands are not yet closely datable but suggest that the higher ridges may have formed an interaction area similar to patterns seen in historical times. Further studies will clarify this tantalizing possibility.

In the Late Bronze (middle and later 2nd millennium BCE) and Iron (early 1st millennium BCE) Ages some specialized maritime-oriented settlements began to appear. The appearance of a port site at Kösk Höyük may parallel the appearance of coastal loci at Istefan (west of Ayancik; French 1986), Demirci plaj (Kassab Tezgör and Tatlican 1997: 354), Akliman, and Sinop kale (citadel) NW, although the chronology of some of these sites is still unclear. At Kösk Höyük and Sinop kale NW the better-dated ceramics suggest that this phenomenon can be associated with the Iron Age. By the early 1st millennium a clear link between the north and south coasts of the Black Sea had been established, as demonstrated at the settlement of Sinop kale NW (Doonan in press; Hiebert et al. in preparation). It appears that the western lobe of the Black Sea was already a flourishing trade zone before the Greek colonial foundations in the 7th century BCE.

Let us now turn to look at precolonial life in three diverse kinds of places—Sinop-Boztepe, along the coasts, and in hinterland areas.

Sinop and Boztepe

Precolonial evidence at Sinop port and on Boztepe is challenging to trace because of the subsequent and continuing occupation here. Although modern construction has exposed clear evidence of Bronze Age activity on Boztepe, no evidence was detected in the Boztepe survey quadrat. The earliest evidence recorded to date for human activity on

Figure 3-3: Sinop kale NW, showing the relationship of the settlement to the north beach landing and the subsequent Hellenistic-Ottoman walls. The upper tower belongs to the Hellenistic phase of the fortifications. The lower tower is an Ottoman extension of the walls that strengthened a secondary entrance into the city. The precolonial site is eroding out of the scarp immediately below the upper Hellenistic tower.

Boztepe was an Early Bronze Age tumulus burial disturbed by the building of the girls' school on the west slopes of Boztepe (Isin 1989). A port has occupied the isthmus at least since the late 2nd–early 1st millennium BCE, before the early Greek colony Sinope was established (Doonan in press; Hiebert et al. in preparation).

An exposed scarp at the northwest corner of the Sinop kale was identified in an opportunistic visit by the Sinop Regional Survey in 1997 (Doonan in press; Doonan et al. 1999; Figures 3-3, 3-4). Excavations documenting a multi-phase Bronze-Iron Age occupation were conducted by the University of Pennsylvania Museum in collaboration with the Sinop Museum in 2000 (Hiebert et al. in preparation).

Figure 3-4: The scarp at Sinop kale NW before excavation, showing several superimposed occupation phases. The stone wall is very similar to examples at precolonial and early colonial settlements on the north coast of the Black Sea.

This settlement overlooks a beach landing exposed to the north, a different situation than the south orientation of the main port in later periods. The exposed section is undoubtedly only a part of a settlement of unknown extent that has been covered over by ancient and modern building. The setting, on the sea and overlooking the sandy isthmus, was certainly not chosen for its agricultural potential. It is well-suited to a maritime-focused economy, possibly including fishing and exchange.

The architecture and ceramics of this site have close parallels to Iron Age and early Classical settlements such as Berezan and Histria in the north and west Black Sea (Doonan in press). The coarse jars with rope like bands and impressed holes or finger marks are particularly widespread in the northern and western Black Sea (Figure 3-5; compare to Solovyov 1999:fig. 20-22). The stone architecture visible in the scarp is very unusual for precolonial Sinop but very common in early colonial settlements in the north (compare to Berezan, Solovyov 1999:fig. 98-99). No Greek ceramics have been found in association with this site despite evidence for an early 7th century BCE Greek colonial foundation in the immediate vicinity, so we may suppose that the occupation precedes the colonial foundation.

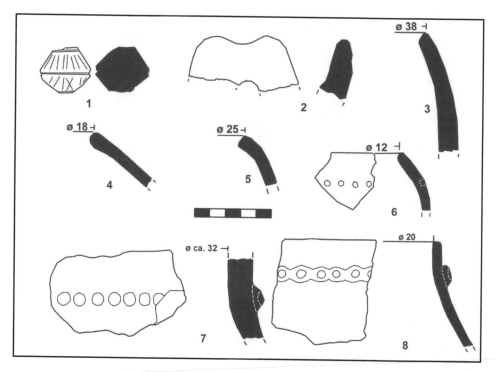

Figure 3-5: Precolonial ceramics from Sinop promontory. (1) Spindle whorl from Kocagöz. Inv. no. 1996-24a.3. Ware: low-fired, chaff-tempered coarse red with incision. (2) Vertical M-shaped handle, Inv. co. 1996-24a.20. Ware: low-fired, chaff-tempered dark brown coarse with burnishing. (3) Large bowl rim from Kocagöz. Inv. no. 1996-24a-4. Ware: low-fired, chaff and lime-tempered coarse red with exterior burnishing. (4) Whole-mouthed jar rim from Kocagöz. Inv. no. 1996-24a.25. Ware: low-fired, chaff-tempered coarse red with exterior burnishing. (5) Large bowl rim from Kocagöz. Inv. no 1996-24a-10. Ware: low-fired, lime-tempered coarse red with no burnishing. (6) Open bowl rim from Sinop Kale NW. Inv. no. 1997-122.9. (7) Large bowl body fragment from Sinop Kale NW. Inv. no. 1997-122.18. Ware: low-fired, chaff-, lime- and feldspar-tempered coarse light brown with exterior burnishing and applied rope like cord decoration. (8) Bowl rim fragment from Sinop kale NW. Inv. no. 1997-122.19. Ware: low-fired, chaff-tempered black with exterior burnishing and applied ropelike cord decoration.

This settlement may be the background behind Herodotus's comment that the Cimmerians (a vaguely known north Pontic group) established a colony at Sinop: "the Cimmerians in their flight from the Scythians into Asia also made a colony on the peninsula where the Greek city of Sinope has since been founded" (*Histories*, IV.12.2). Although the value of Herodotus as a source for the early history of the

Black Sea is dubious and the nature of the Cimmerians as a historical group remains problematic (Ivantchik 2001), Sinop kale NW offers the earliest clear evidence for a port in the Sinop area with close ties across the deepwater north-south sea lanes of the Black Sea.

Precolonial Coastal Places

Human occupation patterns along the coasts of Sinop suggest that the settlement at Sinop kale NW was part of a broader phenomenon of increased coastal settlement. From as early as the 6th millennium the settlements took advantage of the rich plant and animal resources available in the small coastal valleys of the promontory. Braving the dangers of a still-insecure prehistoric ceramic chronology, it appears that coastal settlement expanded during the late 2nd–early 1st millennia BCE (Kösk Höyük- Gerze, Sinop Kale NW, Akliman, Istefan). A strong impulse toward coastal settlement replaced or supplemented a preexisting pattern in which settlements were located near but not on the coast (Kocagöz, Yama tepe, Karaoglan tepe). These coastal settlements are located in places that minimize potential access to agricultural resources and maximize access to the sea. If correct, this view would suggest an emerging maritime orientation (or perhaps a complex maritime-hinterland dichotomy) among the inhabitants of the Sinop region before the establishment of Greek trading networks in the 7th century BCE.

Mezarliktepe is a small settlement on the lower slopes of a coastal ridge at the mouth of the Demirci valley about 15 km south of the port of Sinop port (Isin 1990:253; 1997:99; for location see Figure 3-6). A surface scatter of ceramics and burnt debris about 0.2 ha in extent marked a settlement and industrial area. Evidence of a prehistoric kiln was noted in the form of slag and over-fired ceramic sherds. Geomagnetic investigations in 1999 confirmed that heavy burning took place here, indicating hearths or kilns (Doonan and Gantos in preparation a).

The ceramic assemblage is diverse and may imply Neolithic and Chalcolithic phases (Doonan and Gantos in preparation a). Neolithic phases are suggested by the incised lug-handled ceramics showing stylistic links to types found at 6th millennium settlements in the Marmara region of northwest Turkey, such as Ilipinar (level V A) and Yarimburgaz Cave (level 3) (Doonan and Gantos in preparation a; Bauer 2001). A Chalcolithic horizon at Mezarliktepe is suggested by tripods, convex and bi-convex spindle whorls, and hole-mouthed jars with widespread parallels on the Sinop promontory (Isin 1998; Doonan and Gantos in

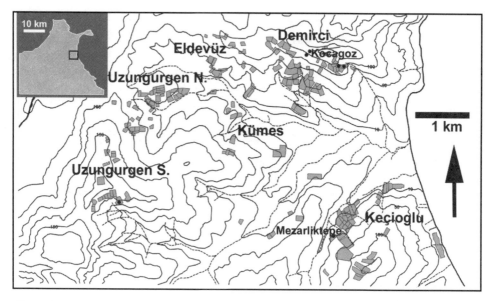

Figure 3-6: Precolonial loci in the Demirci valley.

preparation a). Studies now in progress will clarify if the clays from the valley floor were employed to produce ceramics here.

The ridge screens the settlement from the sea. The marly sandstone bedrock has broken down into sandy soils deposited on the valley floor as alluvial fills. These overlay earlier clays and bay sediments (Kuzucuoglu and Andrieu 1998). Further geomorphological work would clarify the evolution of land forms in this valley, but in the nearby Karasu valley the present colluvial plain has filled in an early Holocene bay (Doonan et al. 2001).

Mezarliktepe may thus have overlooked a small estuary or bay. The presence of spindle whorls implies wool working and animal husbandry as part of the economy at Mezarliktepe. The situation of Yarimburgaz, Ilipinar, and other settlements in near-coastal locations (Özdogan 2000) suggests similar patterns of plant and animal exploitation in Sinop and Marmara.

The Early Bronze Age settlement of Kocagöz in Demirci was first brought to light by the excavations of Ekrem Akurgal and Ludwig Budde in the early 1950s (Akurgal and Budde 1956; Figure 3-7). Burney (1956:184) noted that the ceramic parallels at this site are closer to sites in the west Anatolian–Pontic area than to nearby sites like Ikiztepe, citing examples at Troy I-II and Yortan. This extreme view can

Figure 3-7: The Early Bronze Age mound of Kocagöz höyük.

now be modified thanks to the results of the Ikiztepe excavations (Alkim et al. 1988; Bilgi forthcoming); nevertheless the persistence of a west-Pontic relationship is significant. The clustering of prehistoric sites in prominent locations where both maritime and terrestrial resources can be utilized appears to be a feature of the Early Bronze Age paralleled at Yama tepe and the tumulus on Boztepe. We shall see that inland places offering advantages for communications were also preferred.

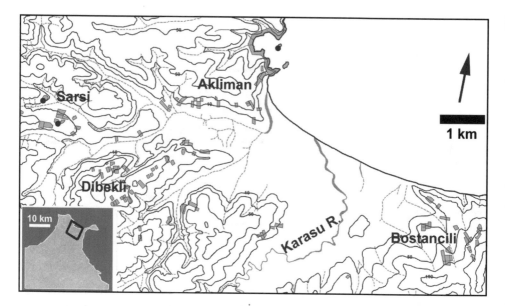

Figure 3-8: Precolonial settlements in the outer Karasu valley.

During the later phases of the Bronze Age a number of coastal places like the one at Sinop kale NW were settled. These settlements have been particularly vulnerable to subsequent building owing to their strategic coastal placement. Kösk höyük in Gerze and the Fener locus at Akliman have both been incorporated into lighthouses (Figure 3-8; also see Figure 1-14); the Sinop kale NW settlement is covered by Hellenistic fills for the city wall and later constructions. Estimates of the extent and organization of these settlements are impossible to make, but their placement directly on the coasts suggests a new maritime orientation among some inhabitants of the promontory. Fishing and exchange are the most likely activities, and it is possible that these were specialized seasonal occupations exploiting the rich annual migrations of mackerel, anchovies, and other species around the Black Sea. The burnished buff wares at Gerze suggest contacts with the Iron Age Kizilirmak delta region, whereas the finds from Sinop kale show strong connections with the north Pontic coast.

Inland Places

Precolonial settlement was widespread on the inland parts of Sinop promontory, particularly on the plains and foothills of the lower mixed marine geological zone. Evidence for the precolonial occupation of the highland flysch zone is more problematic because of the very local hand-made ceramic assemblages of these areas. Although a number of sites in the upper Karasu and Sarimsak çayi drainages have been published by Isin (1998) as Early Bronze Age, it is risky to associate these with partic-ular chronological horizons without farther evidence. Even considering many of these assemblages to be earlier than the foundation of Greek Sinope is problematic, given that these wares show up consistently mixed with Hellenistic and Roman imports from the coast.

We will focus on the fertile central Karasu valley where precolonial settlement was particularly dense and showed a tendency toward con-nection with the wider Black Sea world (Figure 3-9).

The earliest locus recorded in the central Karasu area was Chalcolithic Maltepe in the village of Hacioglu (Burney 1956; Isin 1998). Maltepe is an inland settlement in a small side valley of gently rolling hills just below the eastern ridge of the Karasu valley (Doonan et al. 2001). In contrast to the commanding position occupied by Kocagöz in the Demirci valley, this location does not look out to any known con-temporary settlements or lines of communication. Although several springs are located nearby, the settlement is not well situated to take advantage of coastal resources.

The material assemblage found at Maltepe is exceptionally rich and varied, including evidence for a refined limestone bracelet industry, a chipped stone industry, and ground stone and highly burnished, well-fired ceramics (Doonan et al. 2001). Despite the siting of this important settlement adjacent to the main Karasu valley, no Chalcolithic settle-ments were observed in the main Karasu corridor itself.

The relatively low density of Chalcolithic settlement changed dra-matically in the Early Bronze Age when settlement choices indicate that open sites in areas offering good communications were preferred. Hardly surprising, this trend was accompanied by expanding cultural connections with the western and northern Black Sea.

Gulluavlu is a small (ca. 0.5 ha) multi-phased mound in the Nohutluk district with evidence of human burials and settlement (Figure 3-10). In contrast to Maltepe, the mound is sited out in the open just above the floodplain of the Karasu. At least two cultural phas-es have been exposed by the widening of the Sinop-Erfelek road in 1998.

Packed red daub floors similar to examples excavated at Kocagöz (Akurgal 1956) and Ikiztepe (Bilgi 2001) appear to mark an Early

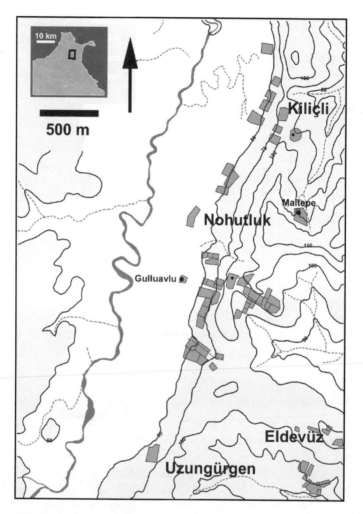

Figure 3-9: Precolonial loci in the central Karasu river valley:
Kiliçli, Maltepe, Nohutluk, Gulluavlu.

Bronze Age habitation phase. The assemblage from this phase reveals
stylistic parallels around the Black Sea, inviting comparison with mid-
3rd–early 2nd millennium BCE sites in Troy II, Karanova VI and the
Catacomb culture in the northern Black Sea (Figure 3-11; Bauer 2001;
Doonan et al. 2001). The second phase is characterized by pitting on the
surface. One of the pits cut by the bulldozer contained an adult burial.
Some of the ceramics associated with the later pitting phase include burnished red wares and spouted vessels closely associated with the early to

Figure 3-10: The Early-Middle Bronze Age settlement of Gulluavlu sits at the edge of the Karasu floodplain, a corridor with extensive precolonial settlement.

middle 2nd millennium ceramics in central Anatolia. These may signal contacts with the coast as well as the other side of the Pontic mountains.

The Sinop Museum's general surveys documented several similar settlements farther south than our survey extended (Habuhas tepe, Kum tepe, Kahkül tepe, and Halil Usta tepesi) (Isin 1998). In keeping with the seeming gregarious nature of the period, these settlements all look onto the Karasu river in what may well have been a chain of communication along this fertile valley. Of course, refined chronological control is required in order to make unequivocal statements about site intervisibility and communications. Although our chronological control is not sufficiently precise at present so we may confidently assert contemporaneity, the pattern here is of choosing settlement locations along an open corridor well suited to local communications and extensive agriculture.

Figure 3-11: Ceramics from Gulluavlu showing connections around the Black Sea. Top center: tripod foot with pin-pricked geometric designs similar to Usatova (Ukraine) types. Top right: raised "eyebrow" relief design reminiscent of 3rd millennium BCE parallels from Troy. Bottom left: red-burnished spouted jug similar to early 2nd millennium BCE types from central Anatolia.

Sinop before Sinope

Some important patterns can be discerned in the precolonial settlement on the Sinop promontory despite a number of problems that remain to be resolved. Up until the Bronze Age widespread communications do not appear to have been a strong factor in choosing settlement sites. The settlement choices in coastal and interior areas tend toward more sheltered sites. We do not presently have enough comparative data to demonstrate whether the presence of industrial debris at Mezarliktepe and Maltepe suggests self-sufficiency or inter-site specialization and exchange. A broader sample of industrial sites from these periods will clarify the economic role of industry in these settlements.

The Early Bronze Age is characterized by a greater emphasis on access to communications in site choice. Settlements like Kocagöz and Gulluavlu were highly visible along land and sea communications routes and took advantage primarily of terrestrial resources. Toward the end of the 2nd millennium communications with the northern Black Sea and central Anatolia became more apparent in the ceramic assemblages, and a strong impulse toward coastal settlement suggests intensified exploitation of maritime resources. The close links between the Sinop kale NW and the north coast of the Black Sea demonstrates that trans-Pontic interactions were already fairly well developed before the establishment of Greek colonies. These patterns may suggest that the pre-conditions for an integrated Pontic economy were already well under way by the time of Greek colonization in the early 1st millennium.

4

Colonizing the Lands of Sinop

The process of colonization is one of the most persistent themes in the history of Sinop port and promontory. Over the past 2.5 millennia settlers from outside the region have repeatedly set up enclaves there. Settling populations included Greeks (late 7th, late 5th and 4th–3rd centuries BCE), Romans (mid-1st century BCE), Turks (12th century CE) and various immigrants from the Balkans and Caucasus (19th–20th centuries CE). Colonies have often formed the basis for Sinop/Sinope's linkage to other Black Sea communities and beyond. In most cases the port was colonized in association with the appearance of new regional authority structures, and the new population subsequently spread into the hinterland.

This chapter looks at the complex process through which Greeks colonized the port and promontory from the 7th to the early 3rd centuries BCE (Figure 4-1). The initial colonial process (late 7th century BCE) did not immediately lead to the engagement of the hinterland. The early colony of Sinope was a strategic foundation along emerging trade routes along the south coast of the Black Sea.

Communities on the promontory had almost no engagement with Sinope or other parts of the Greek world before the 4th century. Only later, when east-west trade routes were disrupted, did Sinope intensify its relationship with the promontory by establishing Greek-related communities along the coast. About the same time Greek trade items began to appear along highland communication routes. By the later Hellenistic

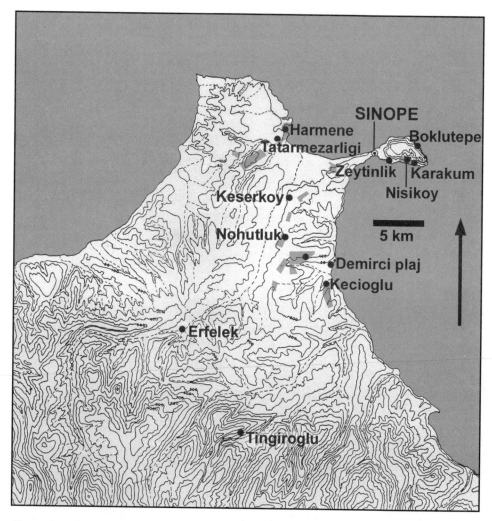

Figure 4-1: Colonial sites on Sinop promontory.

period (2nd century BCE) the promontory was largely an integrated economic and social region with secondary ports and coastal valleys creating an effective interface between the primary port of Sinope and the hinterland. These two phases of colonization linked the hinterland to the Black Sea and Mediterranean economies.

Greeks from the Ionian city of Miletus founded the colony of Sinope in the latter years of the 7th century BCE, documented by historical (Strabo XII.iii.11; Diodorus Siculus, *Historical Library* 14.31.2;

Pseudo-Scymnus 995-96; Eusebius, *Chronographia* 631/30 BCE) and archaeological evidence (Akurgal 1956; Boardman 1991; Tsetskhladze 1994, 1999). The date and circumstances of the foundation of Sinope remains a contentious issue in part owing to the conflicting historical and mythical traditions and because of the pivotal role played by Sinope in the establishment of a Greek trade network in the Black Sea (Doonan in press b). Confusion in Eusebius (*Chronographia* 756 BCE, 631/30 BCE) over the date of the foundation of Sinope's colony Trapezus (modern Trabzon) in the eastern Black Sea has led some scholars to argue that Sinope was founded in the early 8th century BCE (Graham 1983). On the contrary the strong preponderance of archaeological and other historical evidence supports a late 7th century date (Boysal 1959; Hind 1988; Boardman 1991).

Mythological traditions about colony foundations reflect Greek interests in justifying and naturalizing the capture and possession of other lands. Malkin (2001) has argued that myths were one of a number of tools used to create a middle ground between colonists and indigenes, a mythological and cultural synthesis that established a common base for relationships. Myths and heroes were frequently used for this purpose, and they constitute important surviving evidence. The heroes of the *Argo* and other early expeditions associated with the Black Sea represent a kind of middle ground in which Greek-related heroes and episodes were adapted to create a local hybrid mythology.

Marriage between a Greek god or hero and a local goddess or other mythological character can be read as a metaphor for the taming and developing of wild territory (Donoghue 1993). In the myths related to the foundation of Sinope, the nymph/Amazon Sinope successfully resisted the advances of Zeus, king of the gods and of Apollo, the god most associated with colonization (Apollonius Rhodicus, *Argonautica* 944 ff.; Pseudo-Scymnus 986-997; see Ivantchik 1999). Sinope's eternal virginity stands in contrast to other local goddesses who often wed Greek gods (e.g., Cyrene to Apollo in Pindar, *Pythian* 9). The resistance of Sinope may reflect the continued independence of the hinterland of Sinope following the foundation of the colony.

Following the establishment of the Greek colony at Sinope, a series of colonies hopscotched along the southern Pontic coast to the metal-rich belt stretching from Kerasus (modern Giresun) to Phasis (near modern Poti; see Figure 1-1). The colonial port at Sinope was almost exclusively oriented to the sea. No evidence of Greek trading or settlement in the hinterland is evident until the 5th–4th centuries. The

Kumkapi cemetery just west of the Sinop isthmus marked the edge of the early Greek encroachment onto the mainland. Several fine archaic figural stele were found in this area (Akurgal and Budde 1956).

The Greek colonial process extended into the promontory during Hellenistic times (late 4th–early 1st centuries BCE), when many new coastal settlements first showed evidence of Greek-related ceramics. This makes a strong contrast to the situation along other coasts of the Black Sea, such as the outlet of the Bug river near Olbia, where dozens of archaic (6th century) Greek colonial settlements appeared in the hinterland soon after the settlement at the main city site (Solovyov 2001).

The 5th century BCE saw limited expansion of coastal settlement but still very little expansion into the hinterland itself. Xenophon and the Ten Thousand stayed at the port of Harmene 10 km west of Sinope on their journey westward along the Pontic coast back to Greece in 400 BCE (Xenophon, *Anabasis* VI.1.15). Our surveys in the vicinity of Harmene suggest that the port was very limited in extent before Hellenistic times and that there was never any significant development of a supporting hinterland.

From the 4th century BCE onward the melting pot at the port began to embrace indigenous and non-Greek overseas residents, demonstrated by the appearance of the names inscribed on Greek-style columnar tombstones (French 1988, 1988b, 1991). Plutarch (Perikles 20) preserves a tradition that a 600 member Athenian cleruchy, a colony in which participants retain citizen rights in the home city, was founded at Sinope, probably in the mid-430s BCE. Nearly 8% of the burial monuments from Sinope recorded by French identified themselves as Athenian, about the same proportion as those with likely Paphlagonian names (French 1990). The 4th century columnar burial marker of Manes elaiopoles (Manes "the oil seller") records a possible Paphlagonian (or at least non-Greek local) name together with a trade that may suggest a connection with agriculture in the hinterland (French 1990:no. 3).

Control of Pontic trade routes appears to have been key to the economy of Archaic and Classical Sinope. Hecatonymus, the Sinopean ambassador warned Xenophon and the Ten Thousand not to plunder the east Pontic colonies of Kotyora, Kerasos, and Trapezus, linking Sinope's interest directly to the tribute paid to the mother city (Xenophon, *Anabasis* V.5.10). At the same time Sinope was strengthening its influence along the western side of the coast by founding new emporia like Kytoros just west of cape Carambis, a major crossing point for ships across the Black Sea.

The spread of Persian power north of the Pontic mountains disrupted Sinope's control of its eastern colonies. The power balance slipped away from Sinope. The port became a strategic target for ambitious outsiders like the Persian satrap Datames, who attempted to take the city in the early 360s BCE (Polyaenus, *Strategematon* VII.21; Sekunda 1988; Langanella 1989; also see Mithridates II, Pharnaces I discussed below). One response to Sinope's diminished position may have been for a segment of the Sinopean population to emigrate to other Black Sea cities with connections to Sinope, including Olbia and Colchis (Vinogradov 1997; Tsetskhladze and Vnukov 1992). The local economy was refocused on exploiting the hinterland.

The Hellenistic period (late 4th to early 1st centuries BCE) was the political and cultural heyday of Sinope. During the Hellenistic period the landscape was transformed by an expanding settlement distribution and the linkage of local agricultural and industrial production to the international economy of the port. During the 5th century a few Sinopean architectural ceramics are known from Nymphaeum and other cities of the north Pontus (Maksimova 1956). However, during the 4th and 3rd centuries great quantities of Sinopean amphoras began to appear in coastal cities and hinterlands all around the Black Sea (Kacharava 1991; Fedoseev 1992, 1999; Avram 1999; Tsetskhladze 1999b; de Boer 2001). An early 3rd century amphora production facility has been excavated at Zeytinlik on the south coast of Boztepe (Garlan and Tatlican 1998). The widespread exports point to a flourishing port and intensified agricultural production within Sinope's hinterland.

Claims to the landscapes of Sinop promontory were expressed using highly visible cemeteries. Late Classical and Hellenistic tomb monuments just outside the port itself reached spectacular levels of opulence, exemplified by a magnificent lions and stag group from a tomb at Kumkapi excavated by Akurgal and Budde (1956; Budde 1963). Vaulted stone-built chambers were documented at this cemetery in the 19th century, suggesting a grand tradition of tumulus burial in Hellenistic times (Robinson 1905; for a Black Sea Anatolian parallel see Ikiztepe, Alkim et al. 1988). Around Sinope tumulus cemeteries marked the interface between newly claimed Greek-related territories and the interior in several parts of the promontory (see discussion of Harmene/Akliman and Demirci).

The port continued to be a target for ambitious outsiders. Mithridates II attempted to take the town in 220 BCE, prompting its allies from the island of Rhodes to send extraordinary aid, including weapons, military equipment and 10,000 amphoras of wine (Polybius, *History* IV.56). In 183 BCE Sinope fell to Pharnaces I, king of the Pontic kingdom in northern Anatolia, who may have constructed much of the surviving Hellenistic city wall when he shifted the seat of the Pontic Kingdom from Amaseia to Sinope (Polybius, *History* XXIV,10; Livy XL,2,20; Bryer and Winfield 1985). From this point onward the exploitation of the promontory intensified. We will look at these developments in Chapter 5. Through the greater participation in trade, production, and politics Sinope's hinterland became thoroughly integrated into the economy and cultural life of the Hellenistic world. We shall now trace the distinct processes of colonization in three different kinds of places: Sinope and Boztepe, along the coasts, and in the hinterland.

Sinope and Boztepe

The archaeological evidence available to date suggests that the Greek colony at Sinope was founded in the 3rd or 4th quarter of the 7th century BCE (Akurgal 1956; Boysal 1959; Ivantchik 1999). Excavations by Akurgal and Budde from 1951–53 explored many test areas around the city, demonstrating occupation from the late 7th century onward (Akurgal 1956; Budde 1956; Boysal 1959).

The earliest and best-known finds of these early excavations came from the Kumkapi cemetery overlooking the south harbor just on the mainland side of the isthmus. A published series of ceramics clearly establish the presence of a Greek community here by the late 7th/early 6th century BCE (Boysal 1959). The earliest material from the area of what later became the walled town is a deposit of mid-6th century Attic Black figure ceramics that were excavated in a refuse deposit ("bothros") on the north side of the city (Akurgal 1956:49; Budde 1956:6).

The extensive sampling done by Akurgal and Budde in 1951–53 help give us some idea of the organization and development of the ancient town, although unfortunately no plans and few illustrations of excavated material were published (Figure 4-2; Akurgal 1956; Budde 1956). Intact settlement evidence of the Archaic town has not been found to date. Archaic ceramics were found in pits on the north side of town, outside the main occupied area at that time (excavation area "B," Budde 1956:6).

The early settlement is very likely to have been located near the ancient citadel, which until 1998 was a restricted maximum security

Figure 4-2: A 6th-century Attic black-figure kylix from the early excavations in Sinop (photo courtesy of R. Olson).

prison. The closest to this general area that Akurgal and Budde were able to excavate was in the center of town in the garden and around the Pervane medrese (Budde 1956:6–9). In all of these trenches the excavators recorded Classical (5th-4th century BCE) levels, in one case resting on bedrock. These results may point to the significant expansion of the city that would have resulted from the cleruchy established here under Lamachus in the 430s BCE. Six hundred Athenian citizens came to Sinope at this time, ostensibly to replace the followers of the Sinopean tyrant Timesilaus after his expulsion (Surikov 2001). The background context of these events may have been an attempt by Perikles to control this critical node of maritime traffic in the Black Sea and its equally critical local timber resources (Doonan 2002).

Excavations by Akurgal and Budde in 1951–53 documented a small (15 x 8.6 m) 2nd century BCE extramural temple in what is now the Sinop Museum garden (see Chapter 5). Beneath the foundation of the temple so-called Phrygian and Attic Black Figure ceramics, 6th and 5th century architectural terracottas, and small finds dating as far back as the

7th century document the early colony (Budde 1956:5). These deposits beyond the core of the city mark the place of an extramural sanctuary or refuse disposal area (Budde 1956:5–7).

The fortification walls around Sinope, as much as the town's natural situation and other factors, contributed to its long-term preeminence in the southern Black Sea. The fabric of these walls records the rhythms of war and peace in the Black Sea over nearly 2,500 years. The walls created a framework for ethnic and social inclusion and exclusion, a persistent social structure in a town colonized repeatedly over millennia. Walled Sinope remained a political and military center and a target for expanding regional powers through the economic and cultural cycles of integration and fragmentation.

The walls of Sinope were sufficiently established by the early 4th century BCE to frustrate the siege of the breakaway Persian governor Datames (Polyaenus, *Strategematon* VII.21). Bryer and Winfield's (1985:76–79) survey of masonry types in the walls document a significant Hellenistic building phase. The most extensive surviving Hellenistic walls protected the city on the west, blocking access from the mainland just east of the isthmus (Figures 4-3, 4-4). The western wall, vulnerable to attack from the mainland and the sea, was strongly fortified with embossed rectangular masonry bristling with arrow ports. A sea gate provided access to the south port while another impressive gate gave access to the acropolis from the heights above.

The acropolis area and an extension along the south harbor show traces of pre-Byzantine (before the 6th century CE) masonry and may have been the fortified parts of the city before Byzantine times (primarily the western wall across the isthmus and the extension running east from the large northwest tower; see Figure 4-3). The section of the city that Bryer and Winfield (1985: 75-76) have reconstructed as having an ancient grid plan may well have been outside the early walls. Although we might be tempted to connect this grid plan to Hippodamus of Miletus (considered the inventor of classical grid planning), and the Milesian origins of the colony, the grid plan is more likely to have been associated with a later Hellenistic or Roman expansion of the town.

The systematic survey of the south slopes of Boztepe revealed little evidence of Archaic and Classical activity. The Archaic settlement appears to have been compact and almost totally maritime oriented in its interests. No evidence has been documented to date that would suggest a *chora* (an agricultural territory formally associated with a city) or

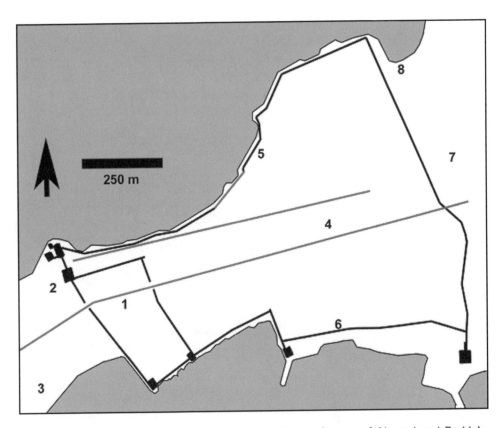

Figure 4-3: Sinop town with the approximate positions of some of Akurgal and Budde's 1951-53 excavations and later research in of Sinop town that have implications for the spread of settlement: (1) early citadel area; (2) Sinop kale NW, site of precolonial port; (3) Kumkapi cemetery; (4) Classical (5th-4th century BCE) houses founded on bedrock, Roman homes with lavish mosaics; (5) Hellenistic earliest domestic occupation; (6) Hellenistic (earliest) and Roman domestic habitation; (7) Hellenistic temple, earlier deposits (sacred?) as early as 7th century BCE; (8) Archaic and later refuse disposal (from Budde 1956; Bryer and Winfield 1985; Doonan forthcoming b).

even extensive farming in the hinterland during archaic times. This pattern contrasts distinctly with that in many agricultural territories of Greek cities in mainland Greece (southern Argolid, van Andels and Runnels 1987; Corinth, Romano 1998), and agricultural colonies (*apoikiai*) in Magna Graecia (Metaponto, Carter 2001) and other Milesian foundations around the Black Sea (Histria, Avram 2001; Olbia, Solovyov 2001). This negative result at Boztepe is based on a

Figure 4-4: The most extensive surviving Hellenistic walls at Sinope protect the port on the landward (west) side. The western city walls pictured here run from the coast at the south port to the crest of the acropolis, marked by a fine gate.

sample of 21 systematically investigated tracts (0.32 km2; Figure 4-5) on the south slopes of Boztepe that yielded widespread evidence for later (Hellenistic, Roman, Byzantine, and Ottoman) occupation. Despite the considerable area restricted from survey because of the active military base, expanding town, and inaccessible topography, this result suggests little pre-Hellenistic development of the suburban *chora* on Boztepe. This is consistent with the model of early Sinope as an emporion, a colonial foundation primarily oriented toward a maritime trade economy.

    This pattern changed significantly in Hellenistic times, when evidence of settlement and industry spread widely over this part of the promontory. The area historically known as Nisiköy is a terrace overlooking a small (ca. 1 km north-south) valley that opens onto the south coast of Boztepe. Limited finds of black-slipped ceramics suggest that

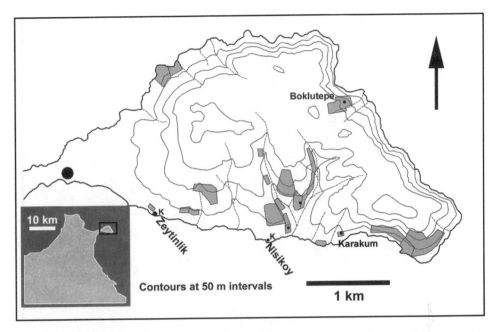

Figure 4-5: Hellenistic settlement on Boztepe. Small (0-0.3 ha), medium (0.3-1.0 ha), and major (5.0+ ha) are indicated. The kiln sites at Zeytinlik and Nisiköy excavated by the French-Turkish team are indicated by "K."

this settlement was occupied from Hellenistic times onward, although the overgrowth at Nisiköy was far too heavy to determine the extent of pre-Ottoman settlement (Figure 4-6).

Another isolated Hellenistic occupation was cut into by a new house foundation overlooking the Karakum beach, several hundred m to the east. Fine and storage wares and abundant cut limestone blocks suggest a structure that was more prosperous than an ordinary farmstead (Figure 4-7). These Hellenistic remains scattered widely (although not uniformly) across the headland suggest dispersed agricultural settlement. A similar pattern has been observed along the coast south of Sinope as well and may point to the expansion of hinterland production following the decline of the city's influence over its colonies to the east (Doonan 2002).

Investigations by a French team in collaboration with the Sinop Regional Museum have yielded important evidence for industrial activity on Boztepe during the Hellenistic period (Garlan and Tatlican 1997, 1998). Excavations of amphora kilns on the south coast at Zeytinlik and Nisiköy have documented intensive amphora production from the early 3rd century BCE.

Figure 4-6: A small Hellenistic settlement at Nisiköy was located on a terrace overlooking a small valley opening out to the south coast of Boztepe.

The amphoras produced in Sinope are widely dispersed around the Black Sea from this period onward, with particularly heavy concentrations appearing in the Crimea and southern Ukraine. The systematic work of Grakov (1929) has been refined by a long series of more recent studies (see Fedoseev 1999: Bibliography). Studies of Sinopean amphora stamps have yielded a rich series of 164 magistrates (*astynomoi*) and 256 potters around Sinope from the early 4th century down to the end of the second. These studies have allowed extensive documentation of Sinopean trade contacts overseas within a precise chronological framework (Fedoseev 1999).

Garlan and Tatlican (1997) have documented the production of several amphora workshops from about 300 BCE at Zeytinlik. Amphora producers here took advantage of local clay and pyroxene deposits to make the black sand tempered amphoras that were the signature of Sinopean trade. The spread of settlement and industry along this coast,

Figure 4-7: The remains of a Hellenistic limestone structure at Karakum were destroyed when the modern house in the background was built. Limestone and ceramic debris can be seen in the foreground.

widespread distribution of Sinopean amphorae from the 4th century onward and ancient testimonia to olive production here all point to the development of an industry here in the 4th century. Perhaps the early expansion of olive production and export was a partnership between Greek colonists and locals like Manes elaiopoles, the oil merchant mentioned above.

Coastal Places

The pattern of colonization along the coasts of Sinop promontory suggests very few minor ports before the Hellenistic period and subsequently rapid expansion. The earliest known Greek-related port along these coasts was the isolated settlement of Harmene (modern Akliman), a

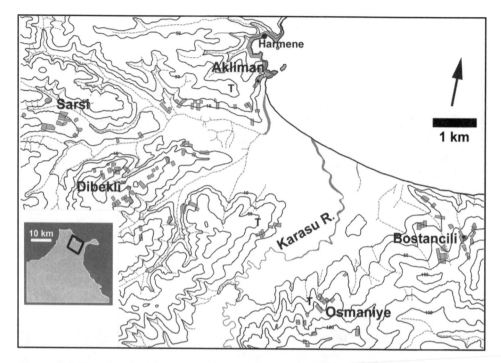

Figure 4-8: Classical-Hellenistic loci in the outer Karasu valley, showing small- (0-0.3 ha) and medium- (0.3-1.0 ha) sized loci. The tumulus cemeteries at Tatarmezarligi, Osmaniye and Karacakese are marked with "T."

small harbor about 10 km west of Sinope. Harmene is mentioned as a minor port in most of the *periploi* (ancient travelers accounts) of the Black Sea. Harmene owed what fame it had to the 5-day stopover made by Xenophon and his army on their return along the south Pontic shore to Greece in 400 BCE (Xenophon, *Anabasis* VI.i.15).

Akliman/Harmene is an attractive natural harbor formed at the interface between the northern volcanic bedrock zone and the Pliocene shallow marine zone characteristic of most of the lower promontory (Figure 4-8; see Chapters 1 and 2). Only 10 km by sea from Sinope, this small port was closely associated with its larger neighbor. Pseudo-Skylax (*Periplus* 89, Muller 1855:I.66) mentioned that the Ocherainos river (modern Karasu) flows into the sea right by the port.

The survey concentrated on the port and a series of tracts along the slopes beneath the Tatarmezarligi ridge (Figure 4-8). The dense forest cover makes it impossible to conduct a systematic survey just inland from the port. Nonetheless, no evidence for occupation has appeared in the road cuts and few other places that offer some visibility suggesting that there was no significant agricultural or industrial hinterland associated with Harmene. The survey tracts along the ridge show almost no evidence of any pre-modern activity (Doonan et al. 2001). The economy of the small port appears to have been totally oriented toward the sea.

The maritime orientation of Harmene is very different from the closely integrated agricultural and industrial production of near coastal areas on Boztepe or in the Demirci valley (see below and Chapter 5). No evidence of industrial activity such as kilns or pressing blocks, has been noted in or around Harmene. It is noteworthy in this respect that Strabo's references to olive production along the Sinope coast are generally limited to the coast toward Amisos, to the south and east of Sinope. The economic differences may in part be due to diverse climate and geology. The Karasu delta is exposed to the north wind that brings rain in the winter, and the sterile sandy soils characteristic of Inceburun and Gerna predominate behind Harmene (Akkan 1975). On the other hand the south side of Boztepe and the coast to the south are sheltered from these winds and feature sandy clays and lime-rich soils.

The only pre-modern evidence of human activity just inland from Harmene is a series of tumuli set on top of the Tatarmezarligi ridge overlooking the sea (Figure 4-9). This area was investigated opportunistically because of the heavy forestation.

Local villagers have disturbed several tumuli in illegal excavations. One of these excavations revealed a burial chamber built of limestone blocks, and the construction technique suggests a Hellenistic date for that particular tumulus (Doonan et al. 1999). The pattern of placing tumuli on top of ridges that have the potential to be seen from long distances (particularly the sea) is reminiscent of other tumulus cemeteries in the Sinop region. This burial type apparently spread from Sinope as Hellenized communities were founded along the coasts. New residents established their connections to local places through these highly visible tombs. The tumulus form may have had particular local resonance because it was so like the prehistoric settlements of Sinop promontory.

The colonial processes in the Demirci valley were very different from those in and around Harmene (Figure 4-10). No evidence has been found of Greek-related settlements in this valley before the 4th century BCE. A dramatic expansion in settlement can be observed during the Hellenistic period. A range of amphorae, mortaria, rouletted red-slipped wares, and other fine ceramics show that the near-coastal (within 3 km)

Figure 4-9: Limestone-block chamber of one of the tumuli from Tatarmezarligi. The chamber dimensions are aproximately 1.5 x 0.8 x 0.8 m.

parts of the Demirci valley were settled as part of a Hellenistic colonial engagement with the hinterland (Figure 4-11).

The clearest indications of Hellenistic settlement in the valley were noted in the Keçioglu and Demirci quadrats, set respectively 1 and 2 km back from the coast. Thick deposits of Roman industrial debris may have obscured evidence for Hellenistic settlement in the mouth of the valley about 1 km to the north.

In the Demirci village Hellenistic settlement extended inland along the ridge about 2 km from the coast. Loci interpreted as settlements were small (up to 0.5 ha) and showed a mix of imported fine wares (Figure 4-11). These appear to have been small farmsteads used as residences as well as production, a pattern similar to the one observed on Boztepe, although the area sampled to date is still relatively small. Unlike on Boztepe one of the problems introduced by expanding rural

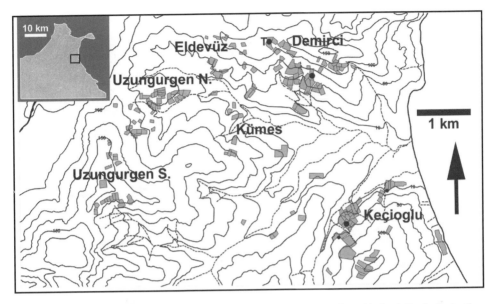

Figure 4-10: Distribution of Hellenistic loci in the Demirci valley. Hellenistic finds in the Demirci valley. Tumuli are marked by "T." Small-sized (0-0.3 ha) loci are marked with smaller dots; medium-sized (0.3-1.0 ha) loci are marked with larger dots.

settlement was the establishment of the territory associated with the new settlers and that of indigenous inhabitants.

Several loci set back 2–3 km from the coast were the remains of tumuli set along the ridge. The siting of these tumuli on top of a prominent ridge easily visible from the sea is reminiscent of the tumulus cemetery in Akliman/Harmene at the mouth of the Karasu river.

Tumuli on the Sinop promontory average about 10 m across and 3–4 m high. One tumulus plowed out for a wheat field was marked by a limestone "mushroom stone" grave monument (Figure 4-12). Dengate (1978:250–51) noted many of these in his survey of Sinop and Samsun provinces in the early 1970s and showed that they were associated particularly with tumuli.

The placement of these tumuli is worth noting, in that they mark a high visible point on the valley landscape. Who was supposed to see them? Behind this simple question lies a subtler problem. Burial markers are active symbolic expressions of social status, and like all symbols their meaning must be understood in the context of new settlement and the establishment of territory in Demirci. There does not appear to have

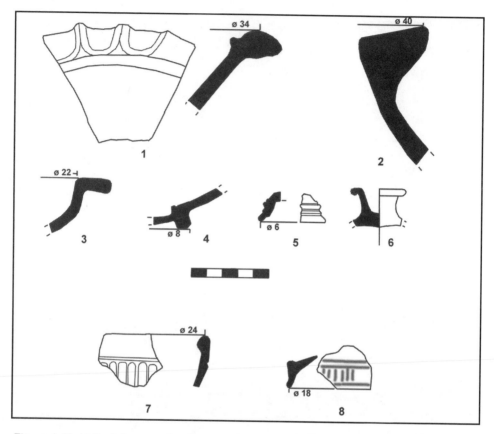

Figure 4-11: Hellenistic ceramics from the Demirci valley. (1) Mortaria rim from Keçioglu. Inv. no. 1997-115g.13 color: 5YR 6/4. Ware: high-fired medium with coarse pyroxene inclusions. (2) Pithos rim from Keçioglu. Inv. no 1997-117c.68 color: 2.5 YR 6/4. High-fired coarse with grog, mica, and lime inclusions. (3) Bowl rim from Keçioglu. Inv. no. 1997-117c.70 color: 5YR 6/4. Ware: high-fired fine burnished. (4) Fish plate from Keçioglu. Inv. no. 1997-115f.9 color: 7.5 YR 6/4. Ware: medium-fired fine with black slip. (5) Cup foot from Keçioglu. Inv. no. 1997-115i.32 color: 5 YR 6/4. Ware: low-fired fine. (6) Lid handle from Keçioglu. Inv. no. 1997-T147.28 Ware: high-fired medium ware with feldspar inclusions. (7) Cup rim from Demirci village. Inv. no. 1997-94.6 color: 10 YR 6/2 Ware: high-fired fine black-slipped. (8) Rouletted rim from Demirci village. Inv. no. 1997.T052.5 color: 5 YR 7/6 Ware: high-fired fine with lime and mica inclusions.

been a clear opposition between Greek and local ethnic identities on the Sinop promontory. The tumulus form had clear resonance with the pre-existing settlement forms on the promontory, and the adoption of this burial type might represent the creation of a "colonial middle ground"

Figure 4-12: Limestone "mushroom stone" grave marker from Demirci.

in Malkin's (2001) sense. We know that most of the south Pontic coast was populated by a wave of mythical Greek argonauts and other heroes (Malkin 2001). The process of creating mythologized connections between Greek and indigenous communities must have been at work in cases that have not by chance survived. The use of a burial type that deliberately mimics local prehistoric settlement forms may reflect this process in a place where local myths are not preserved. This may be analogous to the use of Bronze Age monuments like Mycenae in Greece to establish fictive ancestral claims to territory (Antonaccio 1994). The positioning of cemeteries "behind" coastal settlements might have helped establish sacred boundaries that decreased the potential for conflict (de Polignac 1994).

Inland Places

The central Karasu river valley is one of the few parts of Sinop promontory where we can state confidently that there was local settlement around the time that the Milesians settled at the port. One medium-

Figure 4-13: This multi-period settlement at Nohutluk is set on a terrace overlooking the Karasu river. The settlement spans precolonial and early colonial horizons.

sized (scatter approximately 1 ha) settlement was documented at Nohutluk with handmade ceramics and daub, as well as early–mid 1st millennium and Hellenistic pottery. The settlement is on a terrace overlooking the Karasu river to the west (Figure 4-13). No imported ceramics or other materials have been noted at this locus before the 4th century. Black-slipped fine wares and transport amphorae suggest the engagement of this locus with Greek-related communities from the 4th century onward (Figure 4-14).

To date the survey has conducted preliminary non-systematic investigations of the highlands of Sinop promontory, but some working hypotheses have already begun to emerge. Our investigations to date have concentrated on the upper Karasu river and the upper parts of the Kabali river that empties into the Black Sea on the east coast of the

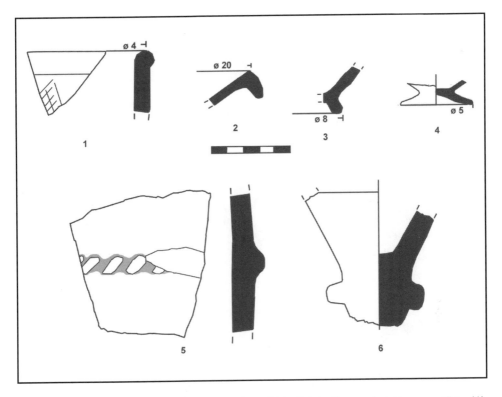

Figure 4-14: Archaic-Hellenistic ceramics from Nohutluk in the central Karasu valley. (1) Straight-sided cup rim. Inv. no 1998-T126.18. Color 7.5 YR 7/8. Ware: medium-fired medium-coarse ware with incision. (2) Bowl rim. Inv. no. 1999-T60.19. Color: 10 YR 5/2. Ware: high-fired fine, no inclusions, black slip. (3) Amphora or bowl foot. Inv. no. 1998-T126.7. Color: 7.5 YR 7/6. Ware: medium-fired with medium pyroxene inclusions. (4) Cup foot. Inv. no. 1998-T126.1. Color: 5 YR 7/6. Ware: high-fired fine, black slip. (5) Large storage jar wall. Inv. no. 1998-T126.54. Color: 5YR 6/6. Ware: medium-fired coarse, calcite inclusions with raised twisted-rope surface decoration. (6) Amphora foot. Inv. no. 1999-T59.11. Color: 5YR 5/8. Ware: high-fired with fine black inclusions, grog.

promontory. The settlement pattern in the Karasu river valley appears to show a break in occupation between the broad valley of the outer promontory and the rougher topography of the flysch highlands. In the rugged middle elevations just above Erfelek sparse short-term episodic use of some ridges was noted. This part of the Karasu drainage is characterized by limited open fields suited for agriculture punctuated by steep flysch outcrops produced by dramatic faulting and folding (Akkan

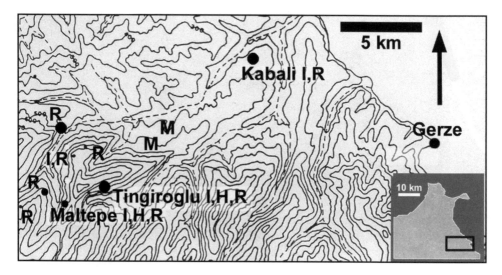

Figure 4-15: Indigenous (I), Hellenistic (H), and Roman (R) settlements in the upper Kabali drainage. Medium (0.3-1 ha), large (1-5 ha) and major (5+ ha) settlements are indicated by smaller and larger dots. Roman milestone findspots are marked by "M."

1975). The very simple local pottery at these loci makes these assemblages difficult to date. These small loci appear to have been temporary in nature rather than longer-term occupations.

In the higher elevations along the ridge tops there appears to be a very different pattern. These ridges offer gentle slopes and greater potential for long-range communications than do the rough valleys below. Local roads frequently follow these ridges and are particularly good in the summer. The survey documented several medium and large settlements (1–5+ ha) in these highlands that suggest extensive settlement from Hellenistic times onward (Figure 4-15).

The opportunistic survey concentrated on a group of highland settlements noted in the upper tributary valleys of the Kabali river. In contrast to the situation in the upper Karasu, large settlements were observed overlooking the deep gorges of the middle elevations. The large (ca. 5 ha) multi-period locus of Tingiroglu overlooks the steep-sided valley of the Kabali river. The settlement is set between agricultural fields and rolling hills to the east and steep forested gorges to the west. Sinopean Hellenistic stamped amphoras from Maltepe 2 km to the south, suggest that this area was in contact with the coast from the 3rd century BCE onward.

Other Hellenistic/ Roman ceramics were made in a pinkish paste with lime inclusions characteristic of this and several other settlements in the Kabali drainage. An isolated and overgrown stone structure was documented at Tingiroglu overlooking the valley. The heavy undergrowth obscures the form and dimensions of the structure, but it may have been a circular stone tower about 4.5 m in diameter. Under the Romans a road that most likely crossed through the mountains was established in this valley (see Chapter 5). The large settlements and tower suggest the valley's strategic importance in pre-Roman times, although it is not clear at what time this structure was built.

Colonization of Sinope and the Promontory

The colonization of Sinop promontory was a complex process that developed over several centuries. From the seventh through the fifth centuries BCE there was very little relationship between the Greeks of the port and the indigenous communities of the promontory. Because of a lack of well-documented chronological evidence our understanding of the nature and density of settlement on the promontory is still unclear. Early evidence of contact between these communities can be observed in the port, the hinterland, and overseas. Fourth century funerary monuments from Sinope suggest that the indigenous population of the port may have been comparable to that of the remnants of the Athenian cleruchy, which had initially numbered about 600.

During the 4th century the spread of Hellenistic ceramics from Sinope and abroad can be observed in settlements along the coasts and along inland communications routes. The coastal regions of the promontory were settled extensively for the first time in the Hellenistic period. Hellenized communities along the coasts may have created a sense of hybrid ancestry when they marked the edges of their settlements with tumulus cemeteries, perhaps consciously evocative of earlier indigenous mounded settlements.

Settlements in the highlands often showed a mixture of Hellenistic imports and indigenous handmade pottery. Dating the indigenous assemblages is still problematic, but it does not appear that upland settlement at this time was as discontinuous as it was along the coast. Continuity would suggest these were native rather than colonial communities in the highlands.

The well-known series of Sinopean stamped amphorae suddenly appeared around the Black Sea in th mid-4th century (Fedoseev 1999), coinciding roughly with the establishment of amphora production facilities on Boztepe (Garlan and Tatlican 1998). We know that several eastern colonies continued to acknowledge Sinope's control until at least 400 BCE, but that less than a generation afterward the powerful Persian satrap Datames not only loosened Sinope's control over its colonies but even threatened to annex the city itself.

One of the most persistent themes in the history of Sinop is the history of ethnic relationships. Hall has shown the value of reorienting studies of ethnicity in the Greek and Roman worlds toward understanding the dynamics of ethnic relationships rather than specifying the identities of ethnic people (Hall 1997:chapters 2–3). Most studies of ethnicity in archaeology have attempted to link particular kinds of things (pots, pins, chipped stone tools) with particular ethnic groups, using change through time as a way of mapping out the conquests and movements of people (Hall 1997).

As one wave of colonists after another has come to this place, some as conquerors, some as traders, each has had to negotiate relationships with a complex indigenous population. The constantly shifting matrix of ethnic relationships in the main port was frequently built around control of the fortified center of the city. In times of danger those in power often occupied the fortified town leaving others to extramural suburbs. In times of peace and plenty the powerful preferred the less-crowded suburbs. In the hinterland similar tensions existed, and in this colonial episode coastal areas were occupied by a mixed Hellenized population who established claims to and boundaries of their territories using cemeteries.

The entangling of the port and promontory through the gradual process of colonization led to the economic integration of the Sinop promontory. By the 2nd century the lands of the promontory were under the control of Sinope, now a leading town of the Pontic Kingdom. The tight economic and political bonds of the late Hellenistic and Roman periods will be considered in the next chapter that examines the industrial landscapes of the promontory.

5

An Industrial Hinterland

The colonization of the coasts set the stage for closer engagement between the port and hinterland (Figure 5-1). The development of an industrial hinterland began during the Hellenistic period, and it is not easy to establish a clear break between the Hellenistic and Roman administrations. Sinope was made the capital of the Pontic Kingdom by Pharnaces following his capture of the city in 183 BCE. Mithridates VI was born in Sinope and had a magnificent palace there (Strabo XII.iii.11; Diodorus, *Historical Library* 14.31.2).

The port flourished as a major center of commerce and production under Roman administration, and settlement expanded widely over the promontory. Following the conquest of Sinope by Lucullus (70 BCE) and the subsequent campaigns of Julius Caesar (47 BCE), the latter founded a Roman colony in the town: Colonia Julia Felix Sinope. A couple of decades after the foundation of the colony Strabo visited the city, remarking on its attractive urban appointments that Lucullus had left intact in taking the city:

> Sinope is beautifully equipped both by nature and by human foresight, for it is situated on the neck of a peninsula, and has on either side of the isthmus harbors and roadsteads and wonderful pelamy-des-fisheries . . . . Higher up, however, and above the city, the ground is fertile and adorned with diversified market-gardens; and especially the suburbs of the city. The city itself is beautifully walled,

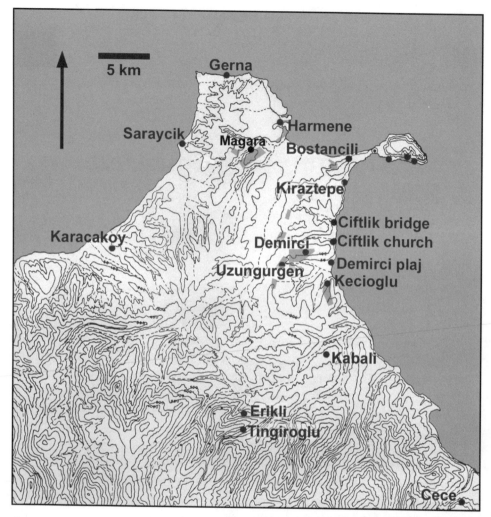

Figure 5-1: Places on the Sinop Promontory mentioned in Chapter 5.

and is also splendidly adorned with gymnasium and market place and colonnades. (XII.iii.11)

St. Phokas of Sinope, patron saint of gardeners, inhabited the beautiful suburban slopes at the entrance to the city where he entertained the Roman troops sent to execute him (Bryer and Winfield 1985). The first bishop of Sinope, Phokas was an avid small-time gardener who is generally portrayed with his shovel, symbolic of the spiritual benefits of gardening.

The olive industry in Sinope may have been the hinterland's primary export in Roman times. Strabo contrasted the plentiful olives of Sinope and Amastris to their absence in other parts of the Black Sea. The extensive olive groves of the coast and timber resources of the hinterland provided Sinope with ample wealth from the hinterland. "The tract of land belonging to Sinope and all the mountainous country as far as Bithynia, situated above the sea-coast, which has been described, furnishes timber of excellent quality for ship-building, and is easily conveyed away. The territory of Sinope produces the maple, and the mountain nut tree, from which wood for tables is cut. The whole country is planted with olive, and cultivation begins a little above the sea coast" (Strabo XII.iii.12).

In addition to these terrestrial riches the fishing around Sinope was renowned. The pelamydes (bonito) was a highly prized catch specifically associated with Sinope, salted and exported to Rome (Strabo VII.vi.2, Pliny, *Natural History* IX.18). Athenaeus (*Banqueting Sophists*, III.118c; VII.307b) praised Sinopean mullets, and several other species are associated with this coast although not Sinope specifically. Aelian's descriptions of fishing practices along the coast suggest groups of ten men working together in coordination to catch the pelamydes (*Animals* XV.10), and about thirty to catch small tuna (*Animals* XV.4–5). Crews of this size could easily be raised in small coastal villages, which filled in most of the coasts of the promontory in Hellenistic and Roman times (Doonan 2002). The profits for the fishing industry were lucrative: Diodorus Siculus (*Historical Library* XXXVII.3.5) records prices as high as 400 drachmai being fetched for jars of salted fish from Sinope.

The city and hinterland prospered greatly under Roman rule, and the products of Sinope's hinterland were distributed widely, based on finds of its Hellenistic-Roman amphoras (Fedoseev 1992, 1999; Vnukov 1993; Avram 1999; de Boer 2001; Kassab Tezgör 1999b). Various forest products (especially nuts), salted fish (especially bonito and mullet), and high-value agricultural products (olives) may have filled the amphoras produced at large industrial installations like Zeytinlik (Garlan and Tatlican 1998) and Demirci plaj (Kassab-Tezgör 1998; Kassab-Tezgör and Tatlican 1998; Doonan 2002).

Settlements were founded even more extensively along the coasts of the Sinop promontory in Roman times, even in places that had little potential to support agricultural production. It is possible that the spread of coastal settlement in marginal areas reflects the new opportunities offered by the integrated Roman economy. It is likely that fishing industries spread out along the coasts in response to the dizzying prices that Sinopean fish earned in Rome. Other opportunities might be afforded by the busy traffic along the shore, such as preying on wrecked-ships, or offering refuge in bad weather (Doonan and Smart 2001; Doonan 2002).

Sinope and the rest of Paphlagonia and Bithynia were brought under direct imperial control under the emperor Trajan in the early 2nd century CE, and grandiose building projects brought about the first real urbanization of many cities of the region at this time (Mitchell 1993:94). An aqueduct project was proposed by Pliny the Younger (*Letters* X.90-91), who was governor under Trajan, although it was probably never built as proposed (Doonan and Gantos forthcoming b). The project proposed by Pliny was to bring water from a source 16 miles from Sinope. Pliny mentioned technical difficulties, particularly a stretch of marshy ground that would have to be bridged. Topographical details in the letter suggest that the source was in the Magara district where the survey documented a series of exploratory cuttings into an aquaferous limestone outcrop (Figure 5-2). No further construction was done at the source, suggesting that the proposal was abandoned.

The road system on the promontory was first organized under the Flavians in the late 1st century CE, to judge from the early milestones (see especially Robinson 1905:77; French 1988:no. 910). French has identified two likely roads that connected the promontory to inland and western coastal regions based on finds of milestones. One road ran along the west coast past modern Ayancik, and the second crossed through the highlands of the Kabali river drainage (French 1988). However connec-tions by sea remained primary, and the strategic importance of Sinope made it the station for the Roman Black Sea fleet, remaining there until the 3rd century CE (Moreau 1959; French 1984; Speidel and French 1986; Mitchell 1993:235).

The transition from the late Roman to early Byzantine periods in the Sinop region appears to have been relatively prosperous. During the 5th and 6th centuries CE churches and villas dotted the coastline of the entire promontory, including two churches at Çiftlik and Bostancili recently excavated by Warwick University in collaboration with the Sinop Museum (Hill 1995, 1998, 1999). The fine mosaics in these extra-urban complexes and a contemporary structure at Kiraztepe (pos-sibly a villa, see below) demonstrate the flourishing economy of the region in these years. The industrial activity at the site of Demirci plaj

Figure 5-2: The exploratory cuttings possibly for a proposed Roman aqueduct at Magara overlooking the Karasu delta.

continued and may have included the processing of olive oil as well as amphora production in later years (Kassab-Tezgör and Tatlican 1998).

Sinope and Boztepe

The Roman and early Byzantine eras (mid-1st century BCE to 7th century CE) corresponded to a remarkable expansion of the town of Sinope, particularly up the hill of Boztepe (Figure 5-3). Strabo (XII.iii.11) mentions that a new part of the city and parts of the agricultural hinterland were given to the Roman colonists. During this period it reached its widest extent and highest population prior to the 20th century, with the urban area covering as much as 3 km2 Akurgal and Budde recorded Roman domestic debris in every quarter of the city, including at several houses with rich mosaics along the north side of

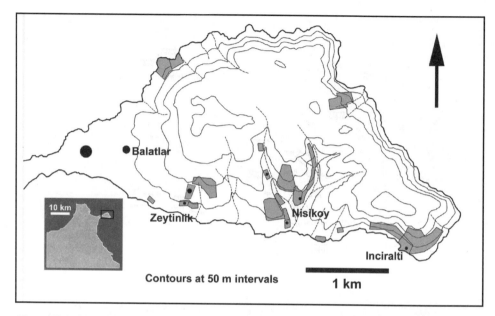

Figure 5-3: Places on Boztepe mentioned in Chapter 5.

Sakarya Caddesi, which was almost certainly the ancient *decumanus* (main east-west street) (Bryer and Winfield 1985; see Figure 4-3). Recent excavations by the Sinop Museum to the south of this same area have turned up more houses with exceptional mosaic floors. Remains of a fine colonnade were excavated in the vicinity of the temple (Budde 1956:7). The population's increased demand for water may have been the motivation for the governor Pliny the Younger to request an aqueduct from the Emperor. Closer water sources from Boztepe and the mainland seem to have solved the problems of the "thirsty colony" (Pliny *Letters* X.90).

Additional evidence for the expansion of the Roman city several hundred meters to the east came from the bulldozing for a new building in 1999). The excavation exposed a Hellenistic phase consisting of a series of large pits with little structural evidence underlying a Roman phase with large stone structures. Although a broader sample is necessary to clarify the general pattern, this limited information is consistent with a pattern of suburban expansion in Roman times.

Half a kilometer to the east, halfway up the slopes of Boztepe, two large monuments testify to the continued prosperity of Sinope through the 7th century or so. A major complex known locally as the "Palace of Mithridates" is situated about a third of the slope up Boztepe overlook-

Figure 5-4: The building complex locally known as Mithridates' Palace (Balatlar) was a large Roman suburban facility with banded brick masonry walls. This may have initially been a bath-gymnasium complex. The core of the complex was converted to a church that remained in use until the 19th century.

ing the town (Figure 5-4). Bryer and Winfield (1985:79-82) have made a strong case for interpreting this complex as initially a 3rd or 4th century CE bath gymnasium complex, based in part on the scale and plan of the structure and in part on the fine banded brick masonry.

A set of large cisterns was constructed just up slope from the complex in a different masonry type, reinforcing the theory that this may have been a bath complex. Each of the three surviving tanks would have had a capacity of about 750 m3 of water (Figure 5-5).

The Roman occupation of the southern slopes of Boztepe appears to have been expanded on the Hellenistic settlement. Wide scatters of ceramics and building debris have been recorded on the terraces overlooking the southern harbor from the Karakum beach into town. Of the 21 tracts surveyed on the southern slopes of Boztepe, 12 had Roman loci and nearly all of them showed some Roman background scatter. Nearer

Figure 5-5: One of four large cisterns about 100 m east (upslope) of the Balatlar complex. The masonry type is different from that of the bath complex and difficult to date.

to town, traces of a single Roman banded brick masonry structure were recorded eroding out of the slopes overlooking the sea. Further investigation of this structure is impossible, given that the building now lies beneath the main road connecting the town to Boztepe.

There is less evidence of industrial activity on Boztepe in Roman times. A recent petrographic study of Sinopean exports in the north Black Sea area has suggested that the predominant clay sources remained consistent from the 4th century BCE to the 2nd century CE (Vnukov 1993). The industrial facility at Demirci produced amphorae from the second half of the 2nd century onward, exporting them widely around the Black Sea (Kassab Tezgör and Tatlican 1998). It may be that in Roman times the primary focus of industrial activity shifted to the east coast of the promontory and that market gardening spread across Boztepe.

Coastal Places: The Coast South of Sinope

The east coast of Sinop promontory arcs gently to the south and east about 35 km from the port. Boztepe is visible from most of the coast, providing a focal point for maritime activities. Since Hellenistic times this coast has maintained the closest relationship of any places on the promontory with the outside world. SRAP conducted a non-intensive survey along the coast from Korucuk to Yali köy. This survey, together with the results of the University of Warwick's excavation of the church at Çiftlik (Hill 1995, 1999) and the French survey for amphora production facilities (Garlan and Kassab Tezgör 1996) suggest extensive Hellenistic settlement and Roman industrial development along this coast.

A Hellenistic/Roman cemetery of tile graves and an elaborate 5th century CE structure were documented at Kiraztepe, about 3 km south of Sinop on a terrace overlooking the coast. Nine tile graves were exposed by a bulldozer cut in a clay fill about 200 m from the coast (locus 96-55). A large 5th century CE structure (locus 96-56) with polychrome mosaics and a monolithic marble column fragment was set on a terrace between the cemetery and the coast (Figure 5-6). The scatter of mosaics, ceramics, and mixed construction debris was turned up by plowing, extending over a 1 ha area (Figure 5-7). Contiguous with this debris scatter on its north side a scatter of pithoi and amphorae marked a likely storage area. The compact nature of the site and its monumental features suggest that this was either a church or a villa. Monolithic columns, a similar ceramic assemblage, and construction debris marked a second structure of similar scale and date 1 km to the north. Marble and limestone blocks have been reused in dozens of houses along this coast. This suggests an unparalleled density of monumental public and luxury private structures in a significant suburban zone. Following this efflorescence this area appears to have become depopulated like other coastal areas outside the fortified town of Sinope. Although findings are necessarily preliminary at this point, it appears that a series of large estates was distributed along this attractive coast during the 5th century or so, some attached to churches and others to villas (Hill 1999).

Demirci Valley

The Demirci valley is our best-documented example of a Roman industrial landscape on the Sinop promontory (Figure 5-8). Roman settle-

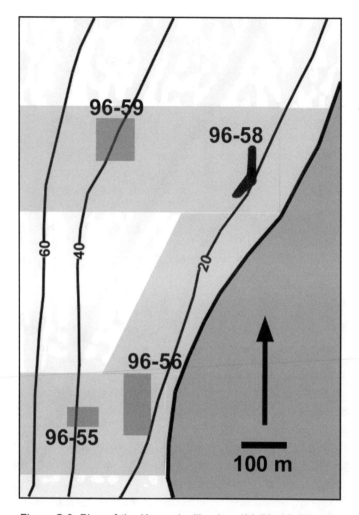

Figure 5-6: Plan of the Korucuk villa sites (96-56, 96-59), the cemetery associated with the Kiraztepe villa (96-55) and an Ottoman battery (96-58). Areas of ceramic scatters are shaded in darker gray. The tracts walked by survey team members (25 m intervals) are indicated in lighter shading.

ment and industrial debris was spread widely across the valley, including extensive scatters of storage vessels, roof tiles, and kiln debris. The focus of this activity was a large industrial installation on the coast at the site of Demirci plaj (Kassab Tezgör and Tatlican 1998). Excavations by Kassab Tezgör in collaboration with the Sinop Museum in the area of

Figure 5-7: Polychrome mosaics (5th century CE) from the Kiraztepe villa.

Demirci plaj have been documenting an extensive amphora production industry dating to the Roman/ early Byzantine period (ca. 2nd–7th centuries CE; Kassab Tezgör 1996; Kassab Tezgör and Tatlican 1998). The site is set on a terrace overlooking the valley outlet from the north. The industrial area extends 0.5 km inland and about 1 km along the coast. From 1994 to 1998 nearly a dozen amphora kilns have been documented here, in what was clearly a major industrial site. The kilns date to Imperial and Late Roman times (late 2nd-6th c. CE; Kassab-Tezgör and Tatlican 1998:440). The excavators have suggested that the site was used as an oil production facility during the 6th-7th centuries, based on the finds of counterweight blocks on-site. Olive pits have been found in amphoras identical to those manufactured at Demirci off the south coast of Boztepe (Kassab-Tezgör 1998). These finds back up the earlier observations by Strabo (1st century BCE) that this coast was given over to olive cultivation.

Keçioglu occupies the ridge pinching in the Demirci valley's outlet from the south. Garlan and Kassab Tezgör (1996) identified several buildings eroding out of coastal scarps of this ridge which might be considered a residential area related to the industrial zone above the valley's mouth. About half of the ridge is cleared for agriculture, although most fields lie fallow and overgrown.

A survey of 37 tracts in the coastal zone yielded the highest density of settlement in the valley for the Hellenistic and Roman periods. The site of Demirci plaj was not surveyed as part of the Sinop Regional Survey's investigations of the valley. Roman settlement was established

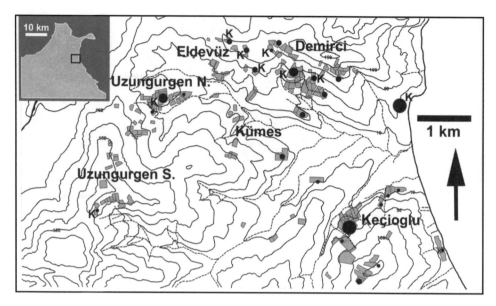

Figure 5-8: Roman settlement in the Demirci valley. Small (0-0.3 ha), medium (0.3-1.0 ha), large (1.0-5.0 ha), and major (5.0+ ha) are indicated by smaller and larger dots. The Demirci plaj industrial area is the major site indicated on the coast. Presence of kiln debris is indicated by "K."

along the top of the Yaliköy ridge. Medium to coarse black-sand-tempered wares predominate, mixed with roof tiles. A series of small loci along the north-facing slope at Keçioglu may represent isolated structures or small farms on the outskirts of the Demirci plaj site. An extensive Hellenistic and Roman settlement was documented on the middle elevations of the northwest-facing slope of the ridge, just out of view of the sea. Fine wares and a combination of domestic and storage vessel and architectural debris, including well-fired brick floor tiles, were strewn over an area of 6 ha. This evidence suggests a standard of residence higher than observed inland.

The ceramic assemblage was varied in forms, with dense clusters of fine wares and large storage vessels. The survey documented the highest proportion of imported fine wares in the valley at Keçioglu. A range of amphorae, mortaria, rouletted red-slipped wares, and other fine ceramics show that the population consumed a variety of imported and high-quality goods (Figure 5-9). Cooking wares, amphorae, and glass finds confirm the site's continued occupation in Roman times, although there appear to be less imported fine wares.

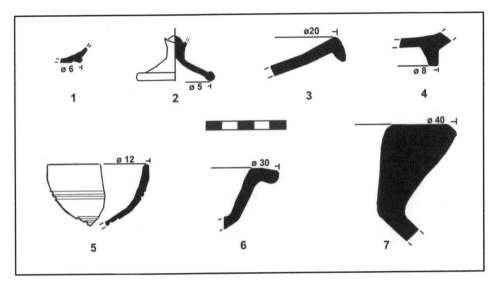

Figure 5-9: Roman ceramics from Keçioglu and Demirci. (1) Cup foot from Keçioglu. Inv. no. 1997-115H.57. Color: 5YR 7/6. Ware: low-fired fine with no inclusions and red slip. (2) Green glass base with rolled rim from Keçioglu. Inv. no. 1997-T149.8. (3) Open dish with everted rim from Keçioglu. Inv. no. 1997-115H.27.Color: 5YR 8/3. Ware: medium-fired ware with no temper, red slip on interior. (4) Ring base from Keçioglu. Inv. no. 1997-115H.54. Color: 5YR 6/6. Ware: High-fired, no inclusions with red slip on exterior. (5) Cup rim from Demirci. Inv. no. 1997-94. Color 5YR 7/6. Ware: medium-fired fine with no temper, incised exterior. (6) Open bowl with everted rim from Keçioglu. Inv. no. 1997-115F.53. Ware: high-fired, no temper, red-slipped exterior. (7) Pithos rim from Keçioglu. Color: 2.5YR 5/6. Ware: high-fired coarse with pyroxene temper.

The interior of the valley was settled extensively in Roman times. Production of ceramics on site is typical of the Demirci valley and has been documented over a dozen loci of ceramic production outside of the large coastal industrial installations. Most commonly tile and pithos wasters but sometimes amphorae, too, were found in association with kiln debris.

A large settlement in Uzungurgen is located at an elevation of 50 m above sea level on a terrace jutting east into the valley (Figure 5-10). From this spot one looks directly along the axis of the valley to the sea. The main scatter covers an area measuring approximately 200 x 200 m, although there are isolated deposits off site that almost certainly relate to this locus. The predominant ceramics at the site include storage vessels and domestic wares in the buff-pink black sand tempered ware typical

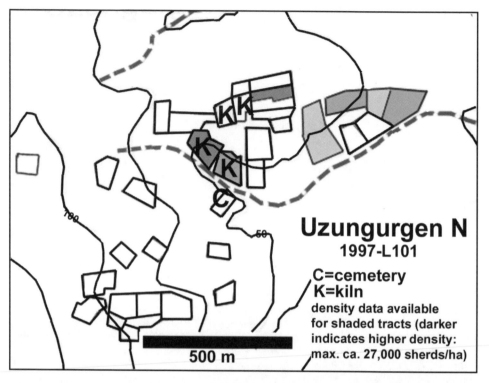

Figure 5-10: Plan of locus 1997-L101 in the Uzungurgen N quadrat, Demirci valley.

of local Sinopean fabrics, with few or no intrusive wares. These ceramics are difficult to date closely, but the settlement appears to coincide with the flourishing of the Demirci plaj and other coastal sites in the late Roman-early Byzantine periods (4th-7th centuries CE) (Figure 5-11). A dense concentration of burnt soil, pithos wasters, roof-tile wasters, slag, and vitrified kiln wall fragments to the south of the main scatter marks a ceramic production area. To the southeast, a scatter of roof tiles without ceramics in a distinct deposit of black organic soil may indicate an outbuilding at the edge of the settlement. About 200 m farther south on the other side of a small ravine a stone sarcophagus and several tile graves have been recently disturbed by plowing, revealing a small cemetery.

An industrial agricultural model is proposed similar to examples that have been recently published from Hellenistic and Roman North Africa (Peacock et al. 1989, 1990; Stone 1998; Fentress 2001). Leptiminus offers a particularly instructive parallel to the industrial-agri-

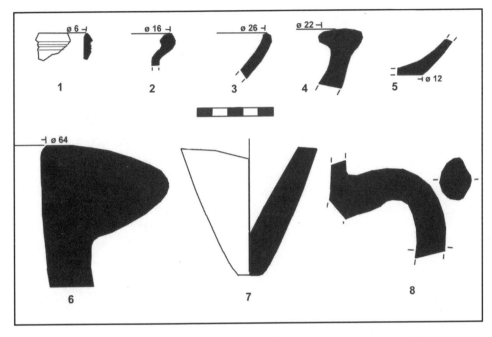

Figure 5-11: Roman ceramics from Uzungurgen. (1) Small cup rim. Inv. no. 1997-T080.38. Color: 7.5YR 7/4. Ware: high-fired fine with fine pyroxene inclusions with ridges on exterior. (2) Small bowl or cup everted ledged rim. Inv. no. 1997-T085.84. Color: 10 YR 5/2. Ware: low-fired coarse with feldspar inclusions. (3) Open bowl rim. Inv. no. 1997-T080.16. Color: 5YR 7/4. Ware: High-fired, red slipped. (4) Coarse bowl rim. Inv. no. 1997-T080.43. Color: 7.5 YR 7/6. Ware: medium-fired with feldspar inclusions. (5) Bowl base. Inv. no. 1997.T080.26. Color: 5YR 6/6. Ware: low-fired coarse with pyroxene and feldspar inclusions. (6) Pithos rim. Inv. no. 1997-101.1 Color: 5YR 7/8. Ware: low-fired coarse with coarse quartz and grog inclusions. (7) Amphora handle. Inv. no. 1997-T080-12. Color: 5YR 7/6. Ware: high-fired medium, fine pyroxene and grog inclusions. (8) Amphora handle. Inv. no. 1997-T080.12. Color: 5YR 7/6. Ware: high-fired medium, fine pyroxene and grog inclusions.

cultural landscape observed in the Demirci valley (Stone 1998). The urban center of Leptiminus is about the same size as the coastal site of Demirci plaj (about 2 km^2), and the suburban zone at Leptiminus yielded 14 Roman sites including 6 farmsteads and 2 possible villas with high-status architectural features (marble, mosaics, hypocaust tiles, and a column base—Stone 1998:307). In Demirci some Hellenistic fine wares were associated with loci as far as 3 km inland, but in Roman times fine imported wares were limited to near-coastal areas. The absence of fine wares from inland on-site and off-site scatters suggests that the inland loci were farmsteads with no elite residential components. These farms may have provided agricultural products, particularly olives, that were packed into amphorae produced at the coastal site and shipped out for Sinope and beyond.

On the other hand the array of fine and imported ceramics from Keçioglu reflects local consumption supported by the profits of local industry. In Hellenistic times those consuming the benefits of exchange seem to have been spread through the occupied parts of the valley. In Roman times it appears that the elite who consumed the profits of Demirci's agriculture resided elsewhere, perhaps in the suburban coastal area or the town. An elite residential quarter has yet to be found in the valley and still may be in an area not yet sampled by our survey. Nevertheless the substantial profits that the valley would have yielded when devoted to olive production are not apparent. Most likely profits were diverted to Sinope, where the elite managing this and other valleys like it along this coast are likely to have been based.

The Coast from Sinope to Inceburun

In strong contrast to the heavy development of the Demirci valley, the coast of the Karasu valley and the volcanic zone from Akliman to Inceburun were sparsely populated in Hellenistic and Roman times. Harmene continued to function as a small isolated port with none of the industrial development either along the coast or inland as has been observed in the Demirci valley.

The single coastal locus identified along this desolate shore was at Gerna, a small cove in the basalt cliffs on the coast about 1 km west of Inceburun (Figure 5-12). The site is currently unoccupied, although local fishermen and hunters frequent it and may be responsible for the illegal excavations here. Gerna is covered in dense macchia and set on a steep rocky north-facing slope. The record of the settlement is necessarily patchy, given the difficult conditions for survey.

Attention was first drawn to the site by a large fragment of a monolithic marble column that had been dislodged and was lying on the pebble beach (Doonan and Smart 2001). Further investigations revealed a half-dozen or more large pits dug into the undergrowth revealing a large brick and stone masonry structure (Figure 5-13). The structure measured approximately 17 m in length and was oriented strictly east to west. The western end of the structure was exposed by three large pits. The

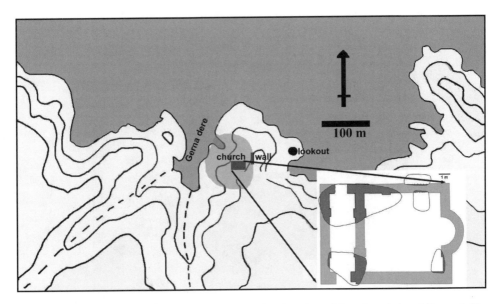

Figure 5-12: Plan of the settlement at Gerna with the plan of the church inset (lower left). The walls revealed by robbers' pits are shaded darker.

masonry is composed of banded brick and stone over a rubble core, comparable to a number of structures in and around Sinope. The Gerna structure is smaller in scale than the Çiftlik church, and the mosaics found at Çiftlik, Bostancili (Hill 1998), and Kiraztepe are not apparent here. The marble column from the beach, the plan, orientation, monumental construction, and scale of the structure all suggest that it was a church. About 25 m northeast of this building a masonry wall was exposed for about 25 m. The wall runs north to south, perpendicular to the axis of the church. This may have been some kind of precinct wall surrounding the church.

Evidence of other structures is scattered sporadically across about 1 km2 wide area, although there is no evidence that this space was densely filled in. A scatter of burnt stone, tile, and other debris may mark a position for signal fires on the Tavsan adasi, a rocky outcrop on the coast about 200 m northwest of the cove.

Poor visibility made it impossible to define any kind of ceramic scatter at Gerna, although some low-fired ceramics and roof tiles were found in the debris produced by the illegal excavations. No closely datable ceramic evidence was associated with the site, and the ceramics belong for the most part to the late Roman/early Byzantine period (4th-7th

Figure 5-13: The church structure uncovered by illegal excavations at the site of Gerna. The banded brick masonry suggests a date roughly contemporary to the late Roman expansion along the south coast and the first phase of the Balatlar complex.

centuries CE). A 2nd century altar bearing an inscription to theos hypsistos and a bronze folles (a Byzantine coin) dated to the 10th–11th century CE are respectively the earliest and latest evidence from the settlement (Doonan and Smart 2001).

The settlement at Gerna is surprisingly long enduring, given that it never seems to have supported a large population or to have acted as a gateway to inland areas. In the 6th century it may have functioned something like Hill's proposed model for Çiftlik: a medium-sized farming estate based on a church or monastery (Hill 1999). The apparent longevity of this settlement may be due to its position on trans-Pontic trade routes. Inceburun, the northernmost point in Anatolia, has been critical to trans-Pontic navigation for millennia. A signal fire on Tavsan adasi could have fulfilled the same function that the lighthouse at Inceburun does today.

The coast from Inceburun to Akliman appears to have been an isolated and desolate part of the Sinop hinterland. The sparse sandy soils of this area offered little opportunity for agriculture, and the harsh climate exposed residents to prevailing winter winds from the north and to the depredations of passing ships, which could bring danger or a windfall to a small community. It is not surprising that to date we have only detected settlement during the Roman-early Byzantine and modern periods, when strong state controls encouraged high shipping volumes and decreased exposure to risks from piracy.

In contrast to the east coast the outer Karasu valley showed very sparse population in Roman times (Figure 5-14). The valley floor was largely swampy and uninhabitable and the few loci identified were set on the ridges overlooking the delta. The ceramic scatter and architectural debris show that the port of Harmene grew into a relatively large settlement but that the hinterland immediately behind it remained largely deserted. A few small loci in Sarsi show that a limited population occupied this area that might have been along a road of some sort that connected Harmene and perhaps Sinope itself to the west coast.

Hinterland Places: The Central Karasu Valley

In contrast to the delta, the interior of the Karasu valley (Figure 5-15) was settled extensively in Roman times. The survey documented several Roman and Byzantine loci in the Hacioglu quadrat including Karapinar, a large (ca. 5 ha) dense scatter of tile and ceramic on a terrace at the watershed of the Karasu and Demirci valleys (Figure 5-16). The ceramics date primarily from the 2nd-3rd centuries CE, somewhat earlier than the Uzungurgen settlement discussed above. This complex settlement included several distinct activity areas (Figure 5-17): (1) a scatter of kiln debris on the north side of the settlement; (2) a concentration of fine table wares documented in tract T99-65 including a the base of a small figurine (Figure 5-18); and (3) a ceme-

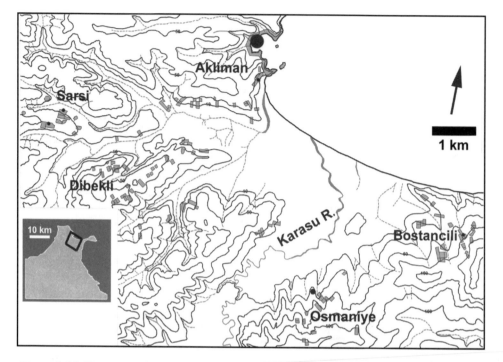

Figure 5-14: Roman settlement in the outer Karasu valley. Small (0-0.3 ha), medium (0.3-1.0 ha), and major (5.0+ ha) loci are indicated by smaller and larger dots.

tery with more than a dozen distinct burial scatters on the eastern slopes.

Storage wares were distributed widely but concentrated mostly in T99-60. Roof tiles were also spread across the settlement and industrial area and appeared in discrete clusters mixed with human bones and limited personal ornaments in the cemetery. The diverse functions represented at this settlement suggest a relatively self-sufficient village or large villa. The fine wares at Karapinar are as high quality as those from any other part of the hinterland and suggest local control of the farmstead as opposed to absentee ownership.

Our sample is still too small to make sweeping generalizations about land tenure in Roman times. Although the picture of coastal and hinterland settlement in Hellenistic and Roman times is becoming clearer, this research raises critical questions about the nature of land tenure during Roman Imperial and late Roman periods (2nd–6th centuries CE). Is the apparent residential-industrial contrast between Karapinar and

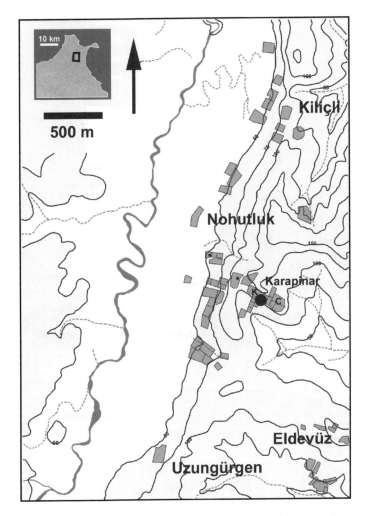

Figure 5-15: Roman settlement in the central Karasu valley, including the Kiliçli and Hacioglu survey quadrats. Small (0-0.3 ha) and major (5.0+ ha) loci are indicated by smaller and larger dots.

Uzungurgen seen at other large settlements as well? Are the differences part of a broader spatial trend with coastal industrial production tied closely to estates or managers in and around Sinope and more independent production inland? Or might the differences be due more to a general shift from Imperial to later Roman times? More extensive research will aim to clarify these questions.

Figure 5-16: The settlement of Karapinar seen from the east. The settlement area is on the terrace near the center of the photograph and the cemetery toward the left (south) end of the terrace.

Highlands

Hellenistic, Roman, and early Byzantine settlement appears to have been widespread along some ridges overlooking the Kabali river nearly up to the watershed (Figure 4-15). This valley system was connected to the coast and Sinope based on a variety of evidence. A remarkable collection of Roman milestones was published by Robinson (1905) and later by French (1988) from the area around Tingir and Erikli mahallesi. Nearly a dozen milestones found reused in various contexts point to the persistent attention paid to this road system through the 3rd century and perhaps a major reorganization under Diocletian and Constantine (late 3rd–early 4th centuries CE). The earliest milestone in this area was found built into the threshold of the mosque in Erikli. It is dated to the time of Vespasian (late 1st century CE) and may thus help

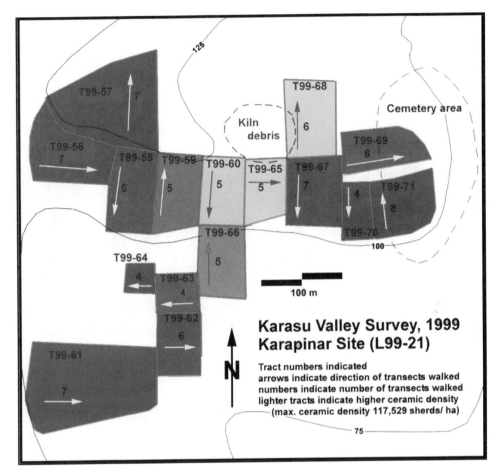

Figure 5-17: Plan of the settlement and cemetery of Karapinar.

to establish when a formal road was defined in this area (French 1988:no. 910). Several of these milestones indicate about 37 Roman miles to Sinope, a clear statement of connection to the port. This distance would be consistent with a road that followed the coast turning inland at the Kabali river and maintaining a track roughly parallel to it. Further finds near the coast at Çeçe suggest that a coastal road continued south and east (French 1988).

As we saw in Chapter 1 highland roads often follow the tops of ridges or pick a path across the middle slopes to avoid the problems of flooding and erosion in the Black Sea highlands. Beyond the obvious question of the precise identification of the path of the road several ques-

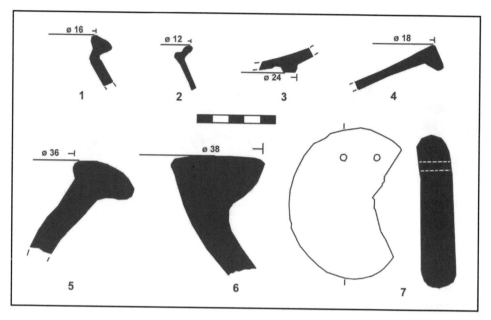

Figure 5-18: Ceramics from the settlement of Karapinar. (1) Globular vessel ledged rim. Inv. no. 1999-T60-17. Color: 5YR 6/8. Ware: high-fired with coarse sand and grog inclusions. (2) Thin-walled cooking pot rim. Inv. no. 1999-T60-22. Color: 5YR 6/6. Ware: medium-fired, mixed sand inclusions. (3) Bowl base. Inv. no. 1999-T60.15. Color: 5 YR 7/6. Ware: high-fired fine, no temper, red slip. (4) Dish rim. Inv. no. 1999-T60.14. Color: 7.5 YR 8/6. Ware: high-fired fine, no temper, red slip. (5) Lekane rim. Inv. no. 1999-T65.14. Color: 7.5 YR 7/6. Ware: medium-fired coarse with pyroxene and grog inclusions. (6) Pithos rim. Inv. no. 1999-T65.13. Color: 5YR 6/6. Ware: high-fired coarse quartz and grog inclusions. (7) Loom weight. Inv. no. 1999-T59.1. Color: 5YR 7/6. Ware: high-fired coarse with pyroxene inclusions.

tions bear on the broader question of its role in structuring communications in the region. How important was this route before its formalization under Roman administration? Did this route pass through the highlands giving access to the major east-west system along the north Anatolian rift valley? And if it did, was it ever used as a major conduit for trade goods that could connect the Sinop promontory to inner Anatolia? On the basis of the evidence presently available this does not appear likely, but it is clear that the efforts to connect the highlands to the coast were relatively successful within the highly integrated Hellenistic and Roman economies.

Sinope and its Industrial Hinterland

The hinterland of Sinope was more closely integrated into the economic and cultural world economy around the Black Sea during Hellenistic and Roman times than at any other pre-modern time. The specialized and integrated nature of regional economies encouraged closer relationships between ecologically diverse regions like the north and south Pontus. Special opportunities afforded by the demand for Sinopean fish and oil promoted extensive settlement in coastal and near-coastal locations.

Based on finds of Sinopean amphoras, the highest volumes of trade seem to have been with the northern Pontus. The relationship between these coasts would have increased demand for the products of the hinterland, including a range of forest-related fruits, nuts, and other products. This may have led to an extensive engagement of interior hinterland areas although our investigations to date are far too limited to make more than tentative suggestions.

The remarkable expansion of settlement and connections was followed by a millennium of withdrawal and isolation for the hinterland in the wake of Arab and Turkish invasions in the 9th–11th centuries.

6

Sinop in the Ages of Black Sea Empires

Thus far we have seen how Sinop and the promontory became entangled with the economic and political spheres of the Mediterranean from the 7th century BCE to the 7th century CE. The middle Byzantine period (8th to 11th centuries CE) was relatively unstable, with Arab and Turkish invasions along the central coast of Black Sea Anatolia (Bryer and Winfield 1985:71). The Seljuks under Izzedin Kaykavus took control of Sinop in the early 13th century. After this Sinop was dominated by the Seljuks of Kastamonu, the Comneni of Trebizond (Trabzon), and other rival regional powers until the conquest by the Ottomans under Mehmet II in 1461 (Figure 6-1). The main port flourished, although there does not appear to have been a closely corresponding expansion in the hinterland. Two European visitors to Sinop in the early 14th century mentioned the locals along the coast who surreptitiously sold high-quality crossbows to passing infidel Christians (Clavio 1928:107; Tafur 1926:129–30). These accounts suggest a certain amount of low-level resistance to the authority of the Seljuk rulers based at the port of Sinop.

These centuries are still historically problematic (Bryer and Winfield 1985), but by the 12th century a new power balance was emerging. Sinop was set in the context of west Asian and Pontic-focused empires rather than part of the Mediterranean periphery. For almost a millennium the Black Sea functioned as a more independent economic unit than it had during Greco-Roman times when the region had been a rich periphery to the Mediterranean core.

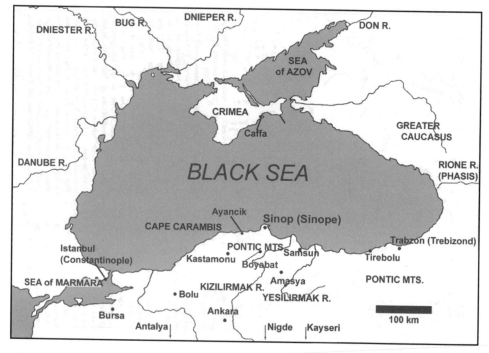

Figure 6-1: Places in Anatolia and the Black Sea mentioned in Chapter 6.

The port of Sinop retained its great strategic value and vulnerability through these years. For the most part the fortunes of the port and those of the hinterland became once again disengaged in the ages of Black Sea empires (Figure 6-2). Raw materials like hemp and wood were sent from the Sinop hinterland to Istanbul (Faroqhi 1984:80). Sinop stood in contrast to most Ottoman towns that functioned as manufacturing centers serving extensive hinterlands (Faroqhi 1984). Shipbuilding, the main industry of the port, was focused on building warships to supply imperial military needs (Yaycioglu in Doonan et al. 1999; Faroqhi 1997).

Sinop's limited engagement with its hinterland is evident in the infrastructure of the city. In most Ottoman towns, bulk raw materials were collected and sold at great covered markets (*bedesten*). Sinop's disengagement from the hinterland in the 16th through mid-19th centuries is reflected in its lack of such a market and unusually small number of shops in comparison to other towns in Anatolia (Faroqhi 1984:26, 39).

Sinop was unusual as a port-town in early Ottoman Anatolia, which was primarily land oriented in terms of production and trade. The only

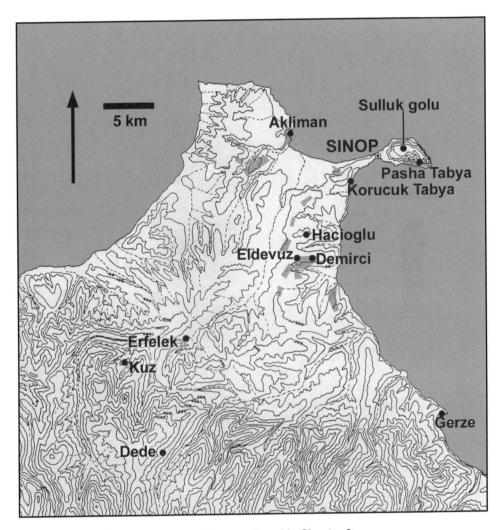

Figure 6-2: Places in Sinop promontory mentioned in Chapter 6.

other early 16th century urban ports were Istanbul, Trabzon, and Antalya (Faroqhi 1984:75). Sinop's function as a port was directed largely toward transshipment of goods to and from the Crimea and east-west from Trabzon to Istanbul. The customs registers of Caffa dating to 1487–90 preserve a remarkable snapshot of trans-Pontic trade in the early Ottoman empire (Inalcik 1995). Sinop was central to this trade.

Exports by merchants from Sinop to Caffa are notable for the variety of goods: iron, copper, tools, textiles (raw mohair, coarse and fine cloth, finished clothing), and leather goods (raw, shoes, and saddles) (Inalcik 1995:121–24). Two of the most valuable cargoes recorded in the registers were from Sinop, bearing textiles (Inalcik 1995:119). More merchants from Sinop were listed than from any other town, including Istanbul (Inalcik 1995:117). Despite the fact that merchants from Sinop dominated the shipping market, their ships carried almost no local products. Sinopean ships were laden with goods from all over Anatolia: Kastamonu, Bursa, Bolu, Amasya, Samsun, Istanbul, Merzifon, Tasköprü, Nigde, Ankara, and others (see Figure 6-1; Inalcik 1995:114-16). Among the most important imports were slaves coming from the northern Black Sea port of Caffa. The usual route for importing slaves was to bring captives from as far as Poland overland to the sea of Azov, ship them to the slave markets of Caffa in the Crimea, thence across the Black Sea to Sinop, and finally on to Istanbul (Fischer 1999:36). Hundreds of thousands of slaves were brought into the Ottoman domain from the late 15th to the late 17th centuries (Fischer 1999:34).

The fortunes of the port became almost entirely dependent on its role in the politics and economy of the Black Sea, while hinterland life became more self-sufficient. Over the 18th and 19th centuries the port appears to have gone into a period of stagnation and decline as political and military instability disrupted trans-Pontic trade (Faroqhi 1984:108).

Following the emergence of more stable political and economic arrangements in the wake of the Turkish-Russian Crimean war (1853-56), the Sinop hinterland once again became more integrated into the more extensive economic and cultural systems. This trend accelerated after the establishment of the Turkish Republic in 1923. Recalling the patterns of Hellenistic and Roman times, the coast to the south of the port became an important producer of a new cash crop, now tobacco instead of olives (Tarkan 1941). Table 6-1 breaks down the major cash crops that were grown in the promontory in the early Republican period (1920s–30s). Note that fresh vegetables were not considered cash crops, although they were widely grown. Fishing and tobacco were primary industries in Sinop and Gerze. Flax was grown in support of sail production as well as for domestic textiles. Cereals and animal husbandry predominated in Boyabat where the continental climate and topography promoted irrigation-based agriculture. Wood was a major source of income in Gerze and Ayancik, where steep coastal mountains offered accessibility to old-growth forests.

The Crimean war brought disaster followed by detente, as an uneasy stability emerged following the establishment of clearer Russian and

Table 6-1: Annual Sources of Cash Revenue from Primary Administrative Districts of Sinop during Early Republican Period (early 20th century)

	Ayancik	Sinop	Gerze	Boyabat
Cereals	—	140,000 kg	850,000 kg	2,160,000 kg
Fresh vegetables	—	—	—	—
Dried vegetables	—	22,000 kg	150,000 kg	50,000 kg
Tobacco	—	300,000 kg	200,000 kg	—
Flax	50,000 kg	3,000 kg	30,000 kg	—
Nuts	—	500,250 kg +10,000 TL	—	20,000 TL
Fruit (arboreal)	1,000 kg	1,200 kg	—	—
Fish	—	30,000 TL	30,000 TL	—
Animal husbandry	—	5,000TL	3500 head	105,000 TL
Leather + wool	—	500 kg + 2700 TL	—	88,000 TL
Wood	500,000 TL	—	2,500 m^3	—
Annual revenue	400,000– 500,000 TL	400,000– 700,000 TL	700,000– 1,000,000 TL	1,000,000+ TL

Commodities denominated in numbers (animals), cubic meters (wood), kilograms, or Turkish Lira (TL)

Turkish spheres. Longstanding Greek communities were replaced by newcomers from the Balkans during the population exchanges of the 1920s (Ladas 1943). Since then, the economy and cultural life of the hinterland has grown steadily more engaged in the Turkish national system. This chapter explores the ruptures and continuities that characterized the region during these turbulent times.

Sinop and Boztepe

Following the florescence of early Byzantine times (up through the 7th century CE) few sources describe the condition of Sinop and its near surroundings before the Seljuk (13th–15th centuries CE) and Ottoman (mid-15th–early 20th centuries) periods. Ibn Battutah passed through Sinop on his way from Anatolia to the Crimea in 1332, describing Sinop with an enthusiasm equaling that of Strabo:

> . . . a superb city which combines fortification with beautification. It is encompassed by sea on all sides but one . . . and it has on that side a single gateway through which no one may enter except by permission of its governor . . . We entered the town and lodged in the hospice of 'Izz al-Din Akhi Chalabi, which is outside the sea gate. From there one can climb up to a mountain projecting into the sea . . . on which there are orchards, cultivated fields, and streams, most of its fruits being figs and grapes. It is an inaccessible mountain that cannot be taken by escalade. On it are eleven villages inhabited by Greek infidels under the government of the Muslims, and on top of it is a hermitage called after al-Khidr and Ilyas which is never without a resident devotee. At the foot of this mountain is the tomb of the pious saint, the Companion Bilal al Hashabh, over which there is a hospice at which food is supplied to wayfarers. (Ibn Battuta, Gibb trans. 1962:465–66)

The praise voiced by Ibn Battuta and others for Sinop during these years is no doubt due to a renaissance that took place under the early Seljuk administration of the city in the 13th century. Sinop was seen as critical to the maintenance of east-west trade routes connecting Persia to the Mediterranean via Trebizond (Trabzon) and Constantinople, and so, the fortifications were strengthened and a magnificent public building program was instituted (Figure 6-3). Ibn Battuta also remarked on the beauty of Sinop's primary mosque, the Alaattin mosque which is one of nearly a dozen major Seljuk monuments still standing in the city (Gibb 1962:466; see Figure 6-4).

In Ottoman times Sinop's fortunes were varied. In the 16th century Sinop became a flourishing center of trade and shipbuilding, but by the early 19th century it was an impoverished backwater. Population figures from the tax records (*tahrir defters*) of 1487, 1530, 1560, and 1582 and later census figures (1890) provide some perspective on the growth of the port in the early years of Ottoman rule and in the 19th century (see Table 6-2; data from Faroqui 1997:654–56; Doonan et al. 1998).

Sinop's old tradition of shipbuilding was promoted into a full-scale industry in the late 16th century following the disastrous Ottoman defeat in 1570 off Lepanto in the Adriatic Sea. In 1571 alone 25 major

Figure 6-3: Walls facing the south harbor of Sinop were strengthened under the building program of Izzedin Kaykavus (1214-1219 CE). The strategic importance of the port of Sinop from the 13th to the 20th century has resulted in repeated reinforcing and expanding of city defenses.

warships were produced in the shipyard of Sinop (Faroqhi 1997). From 1530 to 1582 the population of Sinop increased by 50%. In this later group was a remarkable number of single men who may have come in temporarily as workers (Doonan et al. 1998). The fortified town was divided into 14 Muslim quarters. With the exception of the shipbuilding quarter by the south harbor (Tersane), all 7 Greek quarters were east of the fortified city on Boztepe (Faroqhi 1997; Doonan et al. 2000).

During the 17th century raids by Cossacks ravaged Sinop and much of the southern and western coasts of the Black Sea (Ostapchuck 1990). Travelers passing in the 17th through the 19th centuries remarked on the dilapidated condition of the city (Bryer and Winfield 1985:73–74; Faroqhi 1997). Passing through Sinop in 1836, Hamilton (1842) remarked on the "poverty and privation throughout the peninsula" (I.312). A little more than a decade later (November 30, 1853) Sinop reached its low point when a surprise night attack by the Russian fleet sank most of the Ottoman Royal fleet in the harbor (Figure 6-5).

In Ottoman times (mid-15th–early 20th centuries) Boztepe was, as we have seen, primarily occupied by the Greek residents of the city. The occupation then appears to have been based on small, clustered villages

Figure 6-4: The Pervane medrese and nearby mosque are among nearly a dozen major Seljuk buildings standing in the town today.

widely dispersed over the headland (Figure 6-6). Ibn Battuta remarked on these in the early 14th century (Gibb trans. 1962:466). The shift of Christian populations out of the town onto Boztepe may have happened during the early 13th century, when Çepni Turkmen settlers were introduced following the transfer of control to the Seljuks under Sultan Izzeddin Kaykavus (see summary in Bryer and Winfield 1985:71–73). Boztepe was certainly seen as a less secure place than the city itself, since the residents of these suburbs and villages were allowed to seek refuge within the walls of the city during attacks (Faroqhi 1997, based on the account by Paul of Aleppo in 1658). A small battery (*tabya*) at Karakum protected the south harbor (Figure 6-7).

The so-called Balatlar kilise (discussed above in Chapter 5) is one of a handful of standing monuments on Boztepe testifying to the flourishing Greek community. Part of the complex was converted to a small church, dated by the earliest paintings there to the 9th–11th centuries CE (Bryer and Winfield 1985:87). The church was repainted on several occasions through the Ottoman period and was still in use when Hamilton, visiting in 1836, referred to it as a "modern Greek church" (Figure 6-8; Hamilton 1842:310–11). Bryer and Winfield (1985:81–82)

Table 6-2: Population in Sinop Town, 1487-1890, for Ottoman period

Date	Households	Muslim	Christian	Population
1487	773	597 (2,985*)	176 (880*)	3,865*
1530	611	378 (1,890*)	233 (1,165*)	3,055*
1560	1003	?	?	5,015*
1582	737 (+940)**	504 (2520*)	233 (1165*)	4,645*
1890	1,790	5,041	4,708	9,749

* Populations estimated by multiplying numbers of households by 5.
** Bachelors

suggest that the extensive (ca. 1 ha) complex was adapted for use as an imperial granary in Ottoman times. Another possibility might be that this structure served some function in the slave trade, although excavation is needed to clarify its function in all phases.

Hamilton also visited the Greek village of Nisiköy. Nisiköy was set on a low ridge overlooking the south harbor and a small well-watered valley about 2 km out of town (see Figure 4-6). The place is now overgrown with vegetation, but about 20 small stone Ottoman-period house foundations are still definable, as was the road leading from the village to a small landing on the coast and a spring visited by Hamilton (Hamilton 1842). Our survey investigated the wash in an eroded gully by the side of the settlement in 1999. We recorded ceramics ranging from Hellenistic to Ottoman in date, suggesting that this was one of the most consistently settled places on Boztepe from antiquity onward. On the hill overlooking the village from the north we recorded the stone foundations of a single rectilinear structure (ca. 12 m in length), possibly a dismantled church given its placement and the east-west orientation of its major axis. Not much of this structure is apparent on the surface, nor was it associated with ornamental stonework or ceramics. Other evidence of small-scale settlements on Boztepe was recorded at Inciralti and on the north coast overlooking the old northern port (Figure 6-9).

The most ambitious architectural undertakings on Boztepe during Ottoman times were in response to the Russian attack in November 1853 and the subsequent outbreak of the Crimean War. A large masonry battery was constructed near the present-day Karakum beach in order to supplement the small battery mentioned above. The new battery had emplacements for 11 canons and barracks for troops. The smaller battery is visible in the woodcut from the *Illustrated London News* depicting Sinop harbor after the Russian attack (Figure 6-5). A similar large

Figure 6-5: Panorama of Sinop mainland to the walled town (top) and Boztepe (bottom) from the harbor. Woodcut from the report on the battle of Sinop, Illustrated London News, February 4, 1854. Note how starkly the walled city stands out in the landscape. The tersane (shipyard) can be made out on the far right of the top section. Shipwrecks and fishermen using traditional methods are visible in the harbor. The lower image shows the suburbs of the town rising up Boztepe.

battery was installed on the mainland at Korucuk overlooking the harbor from the south. These batteries together with many hurried repairs to the walls testify to the high priority placed on defense as the Black Sea entered the most militarized phase of its history.

Coastal Places

The coasts of the Sinop promontory became depopulated during the times of the Arab and Turkish invasions (9th–11th centuries CE) and do not seem to have recovered much until the Ottomans came to power in the mid-15th century. The depopulated coasts in these times contrast dramatically with the busy agricultural and industrial landscapes of Hellenistic, Roman, and early Byzantine days. The coastal population expanded under Ottoman administration, possibly beginning with the shipbuilding projects of the later 16th century. Even after the recovery

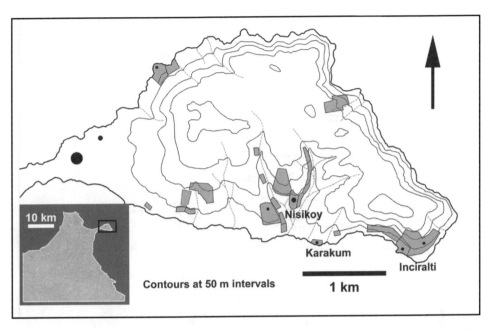

Figure 6-6: Post-antique settlement evidence on Boztepe recorded by the survey in 1999. Small (0-0.3 ha), medium (0.3-1.0 ha), and major (5.0+ ha) loci are indicated by smaller and larger dots.

in Ottoman times, the coastal economy appears to be primarily maritime, in contrast to the Roman–late Roman maritime-industrial-agricultural complex. Rich agricultural production and export seem to have returned in the 19th century with the rise of tobacco production. Two small ports (Gerze and Akliman) illustrate the maritime orientation of the few settlements that were sited directly on the coast.

The small port of Gerze had a strategic position on the coast 25 km south of Sinop. The harbor was protected by a battery on the north side. According to the Kastamonu Tax Register of 1582 Gerze was a center for ship building and repair. Tax documents set standard rates for building or repair of small, medium, and large boats, implying a bustling local industry (Faroqhi 1984:93). Centuries later Hamilton reported busy timber cutting in the upland valleys of this side of Sinop promontory in the 1830s that may have been in support of this industry (Hamilton 1842).

Akliman port was occupied sporadically during these periods (Figure 6-10). The southern island (Sari ada) was the location of a church and a scatter of tile and ceramics. Visibility is fairly low on most

Figure 6-7: The south harbor was defended by this small battery (*tabya*) up until the Russian attack of 1853. This structure can be seen on Figure 6-5.

of the island because of the dense scrub plant cover. The church had a simple apsidal plan, with rather narrow dimensions (16 x 7 m), and was constructed of roughly trimmed, mortared stones (Figure 6-11). Although the southeast corner of the church has now fallen into the sea, the plan of the church is still clear. One close parallel in terms of plan, scale, and masonry is the church at Kilise Burun (Tirebolu), thought to be medieval (Ballance et al. 1966:252–56). Hommage de Hell (1860:344–45) spent a night at Akliman on his 1836 voyage along the Black Sea coast. He described the place as utterly deserted, noting a ruined house but no church. He also noted scattered artillery and wood-working debris that may have been the abandoned remnants of the 16th century ship-building project.

Following Late Roman times the Demirci valley (Figure 6-13) shows almost no evidence of use until the Ottoman period, when trav-

Figure 6-8: Late paintings from the ruined Balatlar Kilise on Boztepe.

elers and tax records show that one or two small communities lingered here building boats. Finds of a few late 19th century Ottoman tobacco pipes at Keçioglu recall the revitalization of this region under tobacco growing around that time (Figure 6-14). Ottoman settlements in coastal areas were most often set back from the coast rather than right near it. The villages of Demirci, Eldevüz, Kümes, and Uzungurgen all illustrate this tendency. By the 1930s Sinop was exporting tobacco to Egypt, Germany, France, and the United States (Tarkan 1941).

Today the Demirci valley is once again the focus of great schemes. The largest industrial park in Sinop province is being built here, notwithstanding the importance of the valley as an archaeological landscape and the obviously unstable land hardly suitable for large buildings. This plan represents the continuation of long-term intensive engagement with Sinop port (now the regional capital) and beyond.

Historical structures do not necessarily imply that a place has the same role all the time. Instead, under given cultural, and social condi-

Figure 6-9: Cuttings for a structure associated with Ottoman ceramics overlooking the point of Inciralti at the southeastern tip of Boztepe.

tions a place might be expected to play parallel roles. This structure emerges out of a combination of topography, resources, infrastructure, and history. Sinop port was a critical transshipment point and military base over millennia in part because of its topography and position and in part because of certain features of its historical development, most notably the city walls. The Demirci valley has tended to have a particularly close relationship with Sinop and the outside world during those

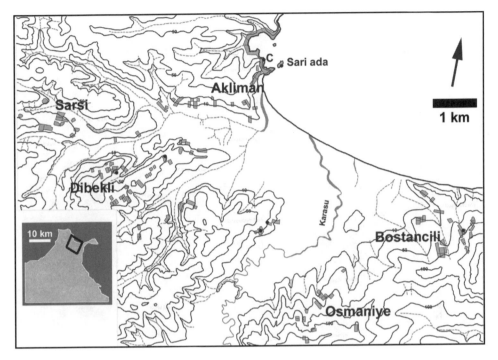

Figure 6-10: Evidence for post-antique settlement in the outer Karasu valley. Small (0-0.3 ha) sites are indicated by dots. The cemetery at Akliman is indicated by "C."

times when the port engaged the hinterland intensively. However, when the economic focus of the port was transshipment of goods around the Black Sea, the valley fell into disuse. This relationship goes beyond simple natural resource distribution. The very clays and pyroxene that were so critical to Roman amphora production were not part of the late Ottoman (tobacco) or modern (industrial park) use of the valley. In fact those same clays may cause landslips undermining the industrial park if the engineers are not careful. The factors conditioning the structure of Demirci's history highlight the importance of resources and topography in the context of Sinop port's economy.

Inland Places

The central Karasu valley appears to have gone into decline like other parts of the promontory during the 8th or 9th centuries and to have been repopulated during Ottoman times. This valley seems to have been

Figure 6-11: The church on Sariada, Akliman.

secluded from the violent swings of fortune on the coast, with people dispersed in small isolated agricultural settlements. This valley was still economically marginal well after the establishment of the Turkish Republic in 1923 (Tarkan 1941), shown by the late establishment of the regional (Ilçe) administrative center at Erfelek in 1961 (Sinop Valiligi 2000).

Several Ottoman loci were noted in the Hacioglu district, suggesting a relatively continuous inhabitation of the terraces overlooking the east bank of the Karasu river. Ottoman villages in this area can be reconstructed based on several surviving examples. They typically consisted of a handful or more farmhouses strung along a ridge or other communication route. One or more outbuildings, kitchen gardens, and household debris scatters surround each house unit (Figure 6-15). The more extensive agricultural fields and pasturage are scattered around the main village cluster. In the Hacioglu district of the central Karasu valley an uneven scatter of roof tiles and ceramics ranging over nearly 1 km suggests that a village occupied the terrace overlooking the river (Figure 6-16).

Up along the crest of the Hacioglu ridge another village came to be settled by a Greek community (formerly Prophitis Ilias:French 1994b).

Figure 6-12: A small muslim cemetery at Akliman.

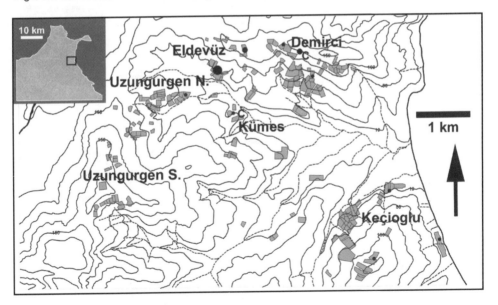

Figure 6-13: Evidence for post-antique settlement in the Demirci valley. Small (0-0.3), medium (0.3-1.0 ha), and major (5.0+ ha) loci are indicated by smaller and larger dots. Cemeteries are indicated by "C."

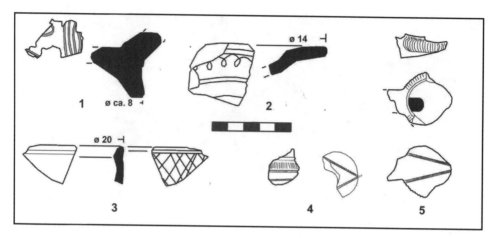

Figure 6-14: Byzantine-Seljuk sgrafitto ware and 19th century tobacco pipes from Boztepe and the Demirci valley. (1) Ring base from a sgrafitto ware bowl, Demirci. Inv. no. 1997-T048.19. Color: 5YR 6/4. Ware: high-fired fine, light green, brown, and yellow glaze. (2) Sgrafitto ware rim from Nisiköy (Boztepe). Inv. no. 1999.T17.17. Color: 5YR 6/2. Ware: medium-fired, no temper, green and yellow glaze, incision filled with dark brown. (3) Sgrafitto ware cup rim from Nisiköy. Color: 5YR 6/2. Ware: medium-fired, no temper, green and yellow glaze, incision filled with dark brown. (4) Ottoman pipe from Keçioglu. Inv. no. 1997-T133.22 Color: 5YR 6/6. Ware: high-fired fine with no temper. (5) Ottoman tobacco pipe from Keçioglu. Inv. no. 1997-112a.35. Color: 2.5YR 4/8. Ware: high-fired fine, burnished exterior.

The Greek-speaking inhabitants were removed to Greece and replaced by Muslim refugees from the Balkans and Caucasus (Ladas 1932). An old church that later became a mosque is now collapsing in the middle of the village (Figure 6-17). This building was converted by adding a minaret (tower from which the call for prayers is sung) and mihrab (interior niche indicating the direction of Mecca) when the Christian residents of the village were replaced by Muslims.

In stark contrast to Hellenistic and Roman times, the highlands appear to have been sparsely populated and rather desolate during Byzantine, Seljuk, and Ottoman times (9th–early 20th centuries). In these later periods the fleeting nature of the evidence and the size and methods of our sampling to date make any conclusive generalizations impossible. Here some cautious proposals might be advanced based on the sparse textual and field data combined with the evidence of extant communities. These proposals need to be tested by future field research.

Figure 6-15: An early house complex in the Sariboga district.

The highlands appear to have been settled in small widely dispersed villages with some influx of population in the summer. The tradition of bringing livestock to upland pastures (*yaylas*) does not have clear origins in the Sinop region. In the eastern Black Sea near Trabzon the tradition of transhumance (seasonal movements between upland and lowland pastures) may be traced back to the days of the empire of Trabzon (Bryer 1975; Bryer and Winfield 1985:7). Each summer far-flung kin come together in the highlands for festivals (*senlik*) where exchange, marriage, and traditional cultural activities reinforce the strength of diaspora communities. For centuries these summer festivals have brought together dispersed communities and provided opportunities to create communal bonds that cross-cut those of lowland winter settlements. In recent times these festivals have taken new ethnic meanings, as local minority groups use them to assert their identities and explore new ways of bridging the gaps between home and diaspora (Figure 1-6; Shami 2000). The organization of valley systems from highlands to coasts based on kinship and

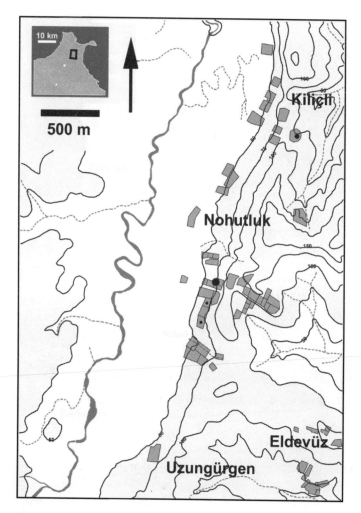

Figure 6-16: Plan of post-antique loci in the central Karasu valley.

political alliances has been demonstrated in parts of the eastern Black Sea region, and this offers a suitable model for testing in the Sinop region as well (Meeker 2001).

The Byzantine and later (9th century CE) religious institutions built on Hellenistic and Roman supraregional cultural and political formations in the highlands. About 2 km south of the town of Erfelek the team documented the remains of a Middle Byzantine church at Kuz Mahallesi, where illicit excavations had turned up a marble relief frag-

Figure 6-17: The church at Hacioglu (formerly Profitis Ilias) was converted to a mosque in the 1920s following the population exchanges that sent Greek villagers to Greece and brought in Turkish Balkan refugees.

ment, perhaps a molding for an iconostasis (Figures 6-18, 6-19). Three rock-cut graves to the north and west of the church had been opened up in addition to a large pit dug into its southeastern corner. It was very difficult to document the locus because of the heavy brush. The walls were of roughly trimmed stone masonry interspersed with brick. Painted plaster fragments, a quatrefoil spout, bossed flat roof tiles with rounded cover tiles and brown-glazed wares suggest a middle Byzantine date (8th–10th centuries CE).

This structure appeared to be isolated rather than part of a larger settlement. The heavy forest growth and peculiarly inhospitable reception by the present inhabitants conspired to frustrate full investigation. Even if this were an isolated monastery it could have functioned as a tangible link to the bishopric at Sinope and a focus of local social order in this part of the upper Karasu basin.

Figure 6-18: Illegal excavations at Kuz mahallesi (Erfelek) have exposed parts of a church structure.

Still higher up in the mountains in the village of Dedeköy a stone and timber mosque established at the site of a local saint's (*dede's*) grave (Figure 6-20). The structure was estimated to be several hundred years old by the caretaker (himself hardly short of his 90s). Associated with this mosque was a guest house and tomb shrine (*turbey*). Our informant assured us that this mosque had served for many villages in the surrounding area in the past, although it seems to be only barely operating today. Similar small mosques have been documented and dated by Kuniholm (2000) using dendrochronology. In many cases these appear to have had similar histories, founded at the tomb of a saint and so the product of peculiar local histories cut off from the world.

Guest houses like the one at Dedeköy provided shelter for the rare travelers who ventured through this remote part of the Sinop highlands. In the early 14th century when the town of Sinop was undergoing a remarkable renaissance Ibn Battuta had to stop overnight "at a hospice in the mountains where there was no habitation" (Gibb trans. 1962:465). Few outsiders ventured into this region, the dangers of

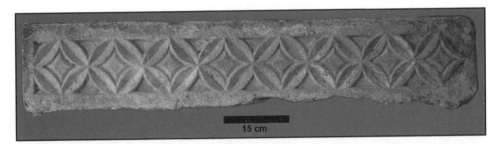

Figure 6-19: Marble relief fragment from the church at Kuz mahallesi (Erfelek), suggesting a Middle Byzantine date (8th-10th century CE) for the church.

Figure 6-20: The early Ottoman mosque at Dedeköy acted as a focal point for widely dispersed villages in the highland region. The complex was furnished with a Saint's tomb (*turbey*) and a small guest house that accommodated the rare passers-by and pilgrims like Ibn Battutah and William Hamilton.

Figure 6-21: The few Ottoman roads that connected Sinop promontory were often little more than tracks marked on their sides by simple graves, as seen in this example from Sarikum.

which were illustrated by the mishap of the Polish merchants who were robbed and murdered in the late 16th century (Faroqhi 1997). Hamilton's experiences on his journey from Sinop to Boyabat in July of 1836 suggest almost no infrastructure supporting transportation in this region and few scattered villages (Figure 6-21). A century later a survey done in the early days of the Turkish Republic shows that timber was the primary contribution of the highlands behind Gerze and Ayancik to the economy of the province (Tarkan 1941). The inland administrative centers of Dikmen and Erfelek had not yet been established, and roads connecting the interior to the coast were limited to the Sinop-Boyabat route.

The emergence of the Black Sea as a political and economic focus under Greek, Turkish, Russian, and other influences highlighted Sinop's critical role in trade and political networks around the Black Sea. For most of a millennium the port remained intensively engaged in the broader

Black Sea world, and the hinterland although nominally under its sway became largely disengaged from Sinop. In the 19th century this situation reversed with the clarification of Turkish and Russian economic and political spheres. This reversal is most obviously seen in the Demirci valley where we see the resurgent production of high-value agricultural and industrial products, recalling the role of this landscape in Hellenistic and Roman times. The re-connection of the highlands to the outside world also revisits a Hellenistic and Roman theme. The ebb and flow of hinterland-coastal-overseas relationships are the local effects of regional processes embedding Black Sea cultural and political relationships in a web of dynamic tensions between integrative and centripetal forces. These forces were brought into sharp focus in relationships between Ottoman, Russian, and other powers over the past 500 years.

7

Synthesizing Places and Landscapes

We have now walked together through many landscape palimpsests and landscapes on the Sinop promontory. Palimpsests are the accumulations through time of human-influenced features in a locale or group of locales. Landscapes are the sets of places that are seen as belonging together by inhabitants in a particular cultural-historical context. Returning repeatedly to a few specific places (Boztepe, Demirci, the Karasu valley) we have seen how inhabitants of diverse locales have been connected with others in distant and near places through social and economic processes. By dividing our discussion along chronological horizons we have been able to make some preliminary judgments about the social and economic systems across the promontory in and between the landscapes under investigation. But this strategy does not consider the evolution of palimpsests in particular places and how the roles of those places evolved and changed under different conditions. This concluding chapter will outline some hypotheses about the evolution of palimpsests in Boztepe, Demirci, and the Karasu valley. Then it will propose some hypotheses about how these landscapes have functioned independently and together in different cultural/economic horizons.

The great contrasts in material patterns from one cultural horizon to another compel us to develop a strategy to compare them to one another. How can we make meaningful comparisons of very different kinds of settlements and material assemblages? A rule of thumb that might successfully define a Roman industrial landscape filled with nucleated villages and outlying farms might be utterly inappropriate to the definition of a prehistoric subsistence landscape with scattered hamlets or dispersed Ottoman villages.

When comparing landscapes of different cultures we must seek a common denominator, a way of sorting evidence that allows us to see patterns through the profuse details. One of the most widely applied strategies in archaeology is to break down settlements based on areal extent (Hodder and Orton 1976). Dividing loci into small (< 0.3 ha), medium (0.3 ha–1.0 ha), large (1.0–5.0 ha), and major (> 5.0 ha) allows us to think about the scale of communities inhabiting each place in different cultural horizons.

Ranking by size provides one lowest common denominator for comparison, but categories must be chosen carefully to highlight meaningful sets. The very different size ranges of settlements in precolonial (almost never over 1 ha) and Hellenistic-Roman (frequently ranging from 1-20 ha) periods require that categories discriminate between relatively small and large settlements in prehistoric as well as Hellenistic-Roman periods. The divisions include a lower range (small-medium) that may help us to distinguish between different kinds of precolonial loci but is less meaningful for the industrial landscapes of Hellenistic and Roman times. The larger divisions (large-major) are less relevant to the precolonial discussion but help to highlight ranking in Hellenistic and later times.

In addition to breaking down loci by size we will highlight special-purpose loci marked as cemeteries and industrial debris separately since they provide clues about the economic and social contexts of life in these places. Industrial loci are counted together with the rest because they nearly always contain debris that might indicate other functions (storage, residence and so on) as well. Cemeteries are tallied separately from the others because they are so functionally distinct and it is difficult to define the spatial extent of common types, like tumulus cemeteries.

Systematic archaeological survey evidence allows us to compare four places we have been following through the volume: Boztepe, the Demirci valley, the Karasu delta, and the central Karasu valley. This comparison provides us with perspective on the immediate environs of the port, two coastal valleys, and an inland valley. Our investigations to date do not allow us to consider the city of Sinop/Sinope or a highland example in this manner, although we anticipate that further fieldwork will provide an opportunity to obtain more systematic data from these areas.

Table 7-1: Density (in loci/km2) of Human Habitation from Systematic Investigations on South Slopes of Boztepe

Period	Small	Medium	Large	Major	Industrial	Cemetery
Pre-colonial	0	0	0	0	0	0
Archaic/ Classical	0	0	0	0	0	0
Hellenistic	12.5	0	0	0	3.1	0
Roman	6.2	6.2	0	0	0	3.1
Byzantine	0	3.1	0	0	0	0
Ottoman	9.3	3.1	0	0	0	0

Total Area Sampled: 0.32 km^2

Boztepe

The headland of Boztepe is one of the most distinctive places on the Sinop promontory, a rocky headland jutting out into the sea, offering great potential to exploit maritime resources and limited opportunities for terrestrial exploitation. The quadrat on the south slopes is one of the few places investigated thus far that has turned up no evidence of pre-colonial settlement (see Table 7-1). Loci noted in opportunistic investigations are not counted. The number of loci in each size and functional category is noted. Industrial loci are tallied with the others although cemeteries are not. Although the systematic survey yielded no evidence of early settlement, it is clear that there was some Early Bronze Age activity on Boztepe and Iron Age settlement on the isthmus, demonstrated by the tumulus on the site of the girls' school and the Sinop kale settlement.

Around the turn of the 1st millennium BCE the small settlement at Sinop kale was the first of many port settlements here. It appears that sailors from the north coast of the Black Sea established the settlement and with it a primary cultural and economic axis of Black Sea history. For 3,000 years the relationship between the north and south coasts has depended on the Sinop-Crimean corridor. The engagement of the port with the promontory often turned on north-south trade relations. The ecological differences between the steppe of the north coast and the mild rainy forests and plains of Sinop form the base of a mutually profitable relationship between these coasts. In periods when trade in raw materials and agricultural commodities along the north-south corridor flourished, the demand for the products of the hinterland encouraged widespread engagement with the international economy. At times when north-south trade ebbed, the communities of the hinterland withdrew from the broader Black Sea economy. Frequently when the north-south relationship declined east-west trade predominated, de-emphasizing the distinctive qualities of the Sinop promontory's ecology.

Following the establishment of an internationally connected port at Sinope in the late 7th century BCE, it took several centuries for Boztepe to emerge as a productive hinterland of the port. Greeks from Miletus established a colony overlooking the southern harbor that in turn established a series of colonial dependencies in the eastern Black Sea. The economy of Sinope depended almost exclusively on these overseas connections, and Greeks cut themselves off from the mainland with a city wall and an impressive cemetery of tumuli. This burial type recalled the form of local precolonial settlements and may have connected Greek settlements in the southern Pontus to communities of fictive ancestors, including the famous heroes of the Argo. The Argonautica was one of the early epic cycles of the Greek age of colonization (8th–7th centuries BCE), associated with Eumelos of Corinth. The tradition of the Golden Fleece of Colchis springs from the association of the eastern Pontus with mineral wealth the distribution of which was largely controlled by Sinope's eastern colonies.

Settlement expanded slowly before the 4th century BCE, when disruptions in Sinope's colonial network in the east Black Sea forced a reorientation of the economy toward local production. Our systematic survey together with the excavations by Garlan and Tatlican documented the spread of farms and industrial facilities across the south slopes of Boztepe in the 4th through 2nd centuries BCE. Visitors like Strabo in the late 1st century BCE praised the attractive market gardens and olive groves of Boztepe. The transport amphoras produced on Boztepe have been found by the thousands at coastal and inland settlements all along the north and west coasts of the Black Sea.

The engagement of the hinterland on the promontory was also well under way at the same time, and in later Hellenistic and Roman times the focus on industrial production slowly moved away from Boztepe. The urban sprawl spread eastward up the slopes and along the coasts. The headland became an attractive suburb with extensive settlement up through early Byzantine times (7th century CE). The density of Hellenistic and Roman small and medium sites reflects the pattern of dispersed market gardens suggested by Strabo.

During the disruptions of the 8th-11th centuries the port of Sinope and Boztepe appear to have gone into a period of decliine. However

Table 7-2a: Evidence of Human Habitation from Systematic Investigations in Coastal Demirci Valley (Keçioglu quadrat)

Period	Small	Medium	Large	Major	Industrial	Cemetery
Pre-colonial	3.1	0	0	0	0	0
Archaic/ Classical	0	0	0	0	0	0
Hellenistic	0	3.1	0	0	0	0
Roman	9.3	6.2	0	3.1	0	0
Byzantine	3.1	0	0	0	0	0
Ottoman	0	3.1	3.1	0	0	0

Total Area Sampled: 0.32 km^2

Sinope's strategic value in the struggles between Byzantium and Trebizond in the 12th–13th centuries returned the city to a position of prominence in the Black Sea. The walls were strengthened considerably in the early 13th century by the Seljuk Alaattin and became a powerful tool of exclusion. Several sources (Ibn Battutah, Paul of Aleppo, the *tahrir defters* of 1560 and 1582) indicate that about a dozen small Greek villages sprang up on Boztepe and the fortified city was almost exclusively Turkish. The small dispersed Ottoman loci on Boztepe reflect this pattern. The city and Boztepe carried on almost totally dependent on the maritime economy for support until the last years of the Ottoman empire and the early Republic (early 20th century CE), when the economic interests of port and hinterland were once again coupled. As in Hellenistic and Roman times the heights of Boztepe have filled in as a residential suburb of the port.

The Demirci Valley

The Demirci valley formed an interface between coastal places with rich maritime opportunities and interior locales with the potential for terrestrial exploitation. We can better understand the way people have inhabited this valley by breaking it into coastal, near coastal, and inland places (see Tables 7-2 a, b, c). People have tended to occupy the coast in situations when maritime opportunities (fishing, trade) can complement or activate the agricultural potential of the interior.

The coastal Keçioglu quadrat showed little evidence of pre-Hellenistic settlement except for a single early settlement tucked behind

Table 7-2b: Evidence of Human Habitation from Systematic Investigations in Central Demirci Valley (Demirci, Eldevüz, and Kümes quadrats)

Period	Small	Medium	Large	Major	Industrial	Cemetery
Pre-colonial	2.9	2.9	0	0	0	0
Archaic/ Classical	0	0	0	0	0	0
Hellenistic	2.9	8.7	0	0	0	5.8
Roman	23.2	5.8	2.9	0	17.4	0
Byzantine	5.8	2.9	0	0	0	0
Ottoman	14.5	0	0	0	0	2.9

Total Area Sampled: 0.34 km^2

the ridge (Mezarliktepe). At least one precolonial site has been noted on the Demirci coast in an area not surveyed by our team, so this generalization will require further investigation.

Greek-related settlements were established on the coast in the fourth century BCE. As at the port, cemeteries were important in negotiating the relationship between new and indigenous communities. Hellenistic tumulus cemeteries have been noted along the north ridge overlooking the valley and the sea (Table 7-2b).

The major industrial site of Demirci plaj is not tallied with these results and must be seen as the primary focus of the economy in Roman (and perhaps Hellenistic) times. Transport amphoras made here were distributed widely around the Black Sea and in parts of the Mediterranean. Pressing blocks excavated from late Roman levels of Demirci plaj may suggest olive processing together with amphora production. In the central and inner valley an extraordinary concentration of small, medium, and large loci (particularly those with industrial debris) suggests intensive agricultural production. The scarcity of fine ceramics and luxury building materials contrasts with suburban coastal areas like Boztepe and Korucuk, suggesting that the profits from this industry were flowing out of the valley. This pattern is most consistent with a model of absentee ownership of agricultural and industrial facilities.

Mattingly (1988) has proposed a working figure of about one olive press per 2 km2 in Roman Libya. Three pressing blocks were excavated by the Franco Turkish team at Demirci plaji and a fourth was recorded by the survey out of context on a farm in Eldevüz (central valley). Four

Table 7-2c: Evidence of Human Habitation from Systematic Investigations in Inner Demirci Valley (Uzungurgen North and South quadrats)

Period	Small	Medium	Large	Major	Industrial	Cemetery
Pre-colonial	0	6.2	0	0	0	0
Archaic/Classical	0	0	0	0	0	0
Hellenistic	0	0	0	0	0	0
Roman	12.4	0	6.2	0	6.2	6.2
Byzantine	0	6.2	0	0	0	0
Ottoman	6.2	0	0	0	0	6.2

Total Area Sampled: 0.16 km^2

presses could adequately serve an area of about 8 km2 (approximately the size of the valley), yielding a maximum of about 20–40,000 liters (750–1500 amphoras) of oil per year (estimates calculated based on rates in Mattingly 1988). The over-all scale of production is far smaller than that of Roman Libya, but the general structure of the Libyan and Sinopean landscapes may not be dissimilar. Productive farms were distributed through interior places, and wealthier villas dotted suburban coastal locales. The three presses excavated at Demirci plaj would correspond to a medium-large farming operation (Kassab Tezgör and Tatlican 1998; compare Mattingly 1988). The evidence currently available is not sufficient to estimate whether the scale of amphora production on the coast was sufficient to supply a larger agricultural hinterland than just the valley itself.

Following the 7th century, settlement and industry in this valley went into decline for many centuries. The slight evidence for occupation suggests small, isolated, and impoverished settlements. This reflects the disengagement of the hinterland from the broader Black Sea economy when the economy and political significance of the port lay in its strategic location and the transshipment of goods between overseas trading partners. In the late 19th and early 20th centuries the development of tobacco agriculture offered a new opportunity to engage in a broader economy. During Republican times this coast has become progressively more involved with the Turkish and world economy, first based on the growth of cash crops and later on industrial development, recalling its Roman efflorescence.

Table 7-3a: Evidence (loci/km2) of Human Habitation from Systematic Investigations in Coastal Karasu Valley (Akliman and Bostancili quadrats, Akliman Harbor)

Period	Small	Medium	Large	Major	Industrial	Cemetery
Pre-colonial	2.5	0	0	0	0	0
Archaic/Classical	2.5	0	0	0	0	0
Hellenistic	0	5	0	0	0	2.5
Roman	0	5	2.5	0	0	2.5
Byzantine	0	2.5	0	0	0	0
Ottoman	2.5	2.5	0	0	0	2.5

Total Area Sampled: 0.40 km^2

The Karasu Valley

The Karasu valley survey provides a second case study of a coastal valley and of an inland river valley (Table 7-3 a-c). The outer Karasu valley (coastal and delta areas) shows a remarkable contrast to the Demirci valley in post-colonial periods. In the Bronze Age the pattern in the outer Karasu was similar to Demirci, with sparse small settlements overlooking the valley floor. These were situated in places that could offer hunting, gathering, and agricultural resources and were close enough to the coast to offer access to rich seasonal fishing opportunities. The small locus on Karaada is similar in setting and ceramic assemblages to other maritime loci at Gerze, Sinop kale NW and other settlements. These may reflect the increasing importance of maritime resources and communications just before the Greek colonial episode.

The small port of Harmene was one of the earliest Greek foundations on the promontory outside of Sinope itself. Despite the early foundation, no industrial-agricultural economy developed in its hinterland. In all pre-modern times the slopes overlooking the Karasu delta were characterized by sparse, small-scale settlement, and subsistence-level economy. The small port of Harmene/Akliman was occupied during most cultural horizons, but it never grew larger than a modest fishing hamlet.

The central Karasu was more consistently and densely settled in most periods. Widespread and relatively dense Bronze Age settlement may have taken advantage of good communications and the fertility of

Table 7-3b: Evidence (loci/km2) of Human Habitation from Systematic Investigations in the Slopes Overlooking Karasu Delta (Sarsi, Dibekli, and Osmaniye quadrats)

Period	Small	Medium	Large	Major	Industrial	Cemetery
Pre-colonial	6.9	0	0	0	0	0
Archaic/ Classical	0	0	0	0	0	0
Hellenistic	0	0	0	0	0	4.6
Roman	2.3	4.6	0	0	0	0
Byzantine	0	0	0	0	0	0
Ottoman	0	4.6	0	0	0	0

Total Area Sampled: 0.43 km^2

the broad river valley. Indigenous settlement in one medium-sized locus (Nohutluk) shows continuity up to the Hellenistic colonization of the coasts. Hellenistic amphoras produced on Boztepe appeared in limited quantities here along with other Greek ceramics. This appears to be an indigenous settlement with links to the coastal colonists rather than an inland colonial site.

The Roman village or large villa at Karapinar is located about 200 m to the south of the Nohutluk locus, suggesting continuity. The assemblage at Karapinar is more suggestive of an owner-occupied settlement than an absentee-owned farming installation, in contrast to the model proposed for the Demirci valley. The Roman central Karasu valley was inhabited as densely as the Demirci valley, suggesting widespread agriculture. Further systematic survey is planned that will connect the east and west coasts to the central Karasu valley to determine if a patchwork of indigenous independent farms in the interior contrasts with dependent industrial production along the coasts.

The evidence of later periods implies a more or less deserted landscape until Ottoman times when once again a rather high density of loci appears along the north-south running ridge flanking the valley on the east in roughly the same area of dense Roman settlement. The material assemblages are simple and consistent with the information from early Republican economic and administrative sources that suggest an isolated, subsistence economy (Tarkan 1941). The area remained underdeveloped until the founding of the administrative district capital of Erfelek in 1961 (Sinop valiligi 2000).

Table 7-3c: Evidence (loci/km2) of Human Habitation from Systematic Investigations in Inner Karasu Valley (Kiliçli and Hacioglu quadrats)

Period	Small	Medium	Large	Major	Industrial	Cemetery
Pre-colonial	0	16.2	0	0	0	0
Archaic/ Classical	0	5.4	0	0	0	0
Hellenistic	0	5.4	0	0	0	0
Roman	10.8	0	5.4	5.4	5.4	5.4
Byzantine	0	0	0	0	0	0
Ottoman	5.4	5.4	10.8	0	0	0

Total Area Sampled: 0.19 km^2

The Highlands

The highlands remain less explored than the places discussed above. Any proposals about economic and cultural patterns here would be very tentative before we have conducted systematic surveys in this area. Nevertheless I will hazard a couple of preliminary hypotheses about this region based on opportunistic results and written sources. The hypotheses advanced below pertain specifically to the highlands overlooking the Kabali river, discussed above.

The rhythms of life in the highlands seem to have been just as closely tied to the prevailing economic trends at the port as were those in the lower parts of the promontory. Settlements we have investigated in pre-Hellenistic and post-Roman horizons tend to be small and isolated in their material assemblages. This pattern typifies those horizons in which the port was engaged primarily in managing trade through the Black Sea (precolonial, early colonial, later Byzantine-Ottoman). On the other hand connections between the coast and the highlands are more apparent in those horizons when the port-hinterland relationship was closer (Hellenistic-Roman, modern).

The Romans apparently maintained a road along the flanks of the Kabali river that connected highland plateaus to the coast. It is unclear whether this road cut through the mountains, but it is unlikely that it was a significant artery for high-volume long-distance trade connecting the inland road along the north Anatolian fault to the coast. The hypothesis that the communities north of the watershed of the central Pontic coastal mountains were largely isolated from their neighbors to

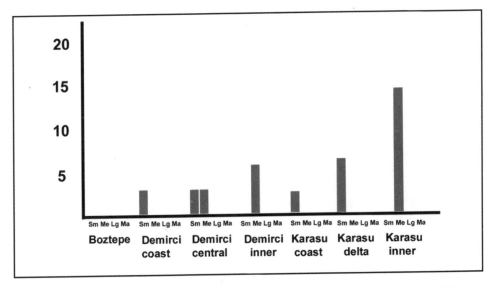

Figure 7-1: Precolonial settlement frequency on Boztepe and in the Demirci and Karasu valleys.

the south remains to be tested by field results. Anecdotal evidence from Ottoman times suggests that the highlands were isolated and crossed at peril. Local religious institutions may have provided some degree of shelter and organization in this desolate landscape, but not sufficient to support significant trade.

Synthesizing Landscapes

The Sinop promontory can be considered as a unit as well as broken into the places we have discussed above. The places investigated by our quadrat survey to date can be broken into three categories (patch types) based on economic potential: coastal (Boztepe, Demirci coast, Karasu coast), near coastal (Central Demirci, Karasu delta), and inland (Inner Demirci, Inner Karasu). By comparing data from these three patch types hypotheses can be formed about the roles different patches played in the economic organization of the promontory.

The precolonial horizon shows a persistent pattern of dispersed small-scale settlement with little trace of settlement hierarchy (Figure 7-1). All of the loci identified to date fall into the small and medium categories, and no locus is a serious candidate for being a regional center. Neolithic and Chalcolithic evidence are too sparse for patterns to be

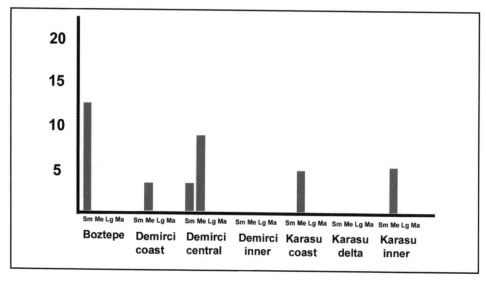

Figure 7-2: Hellenistic settlement frequency on Boztepe and in the Demirci and Karasu valleys.

apparent as yet, but there appears to have been some preference for near coastal and inland settlement locations.

The limited evidence for coastal settlement in the Demirci valley is based on the presence of Mezarliktepe, a Neolithic settlement that was not really coastal as it overlooked a small estuary but was sheltered from the coast itself. In the Karasu valley the evidence of coastal settlement at Karaada is related to a phenomenon of Iron Age coastal settlement, as yet only slightly documented by the survey. The dispersed non-hierarchical pattern in hinterland settlement continued after the foundation of Sinope.

An expansion of small and medium-sized settlements in coastal and near-coastal patches can be observed in Hellenistic times (4th-2nd centuries BCE) (Figure 7-2). The pattern is particularly striking on Boztepe and in the Demirci valley. This new pattern coincides with the use of Greek ceramics and probably represents an influx of either Greek settlers or a mix of Greek and local inhabitants. The settlement in the interior of the Karasu valley continues from precolonial times and may represent the economic engagement of indigenous communities.

The late Roman and early Byzantine landscapes (4th–7th centuries CE) show an extraordinary expansion in settlement density in all areas and the emergence of hierarchies in terms of size (Figure 7-3). The most

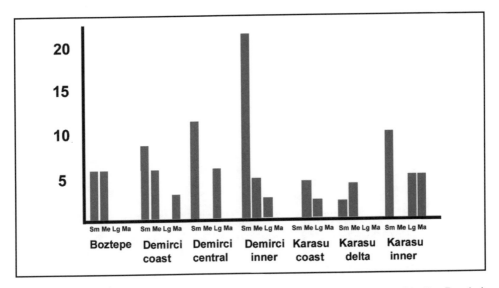

Figure 7-3: Roman and late Roman settlement frequency on Boztepe and in the Demirci and Karasu valleys.

dramatic rise in density was in the Demirci valley, where we have already noted evidence for the emergence of industrial-scale olive production. The high densities of settlements in near-coastal and inland patches suggest extensive agricultural production. What is missing from the distribution is the major industrial site of Demirci plaj on the coast, the key to understanding the Roman economy of the valley.

The shrinkage of hinterland settlement in later Byzantine and Seljuk periods (8th–15th centuries CE) is as striking as the expansion in Roman times (Figure 7-4). These times represent a collapse in the settlement of the hinterland and the exaggerated importance of the port itself. The city walls of Sinop were expanded significantly, particularly under Seljuk administration (13th–15th centuries CE). The increased population of Sinop port was most likely due to the insecurity of life outside the protected citadel as rival Arab, Greek, and Turkish groups vied for control of the critical central Black Sea region.

Ottoman times witnessed the rebound of hinterland settlement, particularly on Boztepe and in near-coastal and inland patches (Figure 7-5). According to written sources Boztepe was settled in a dozen or more Greek districts, which can be seen in the dispersed small loci there.

On the mainland coastal settlement remained limited but near the coasts and inland a more dispersed settlement pattern developed. The

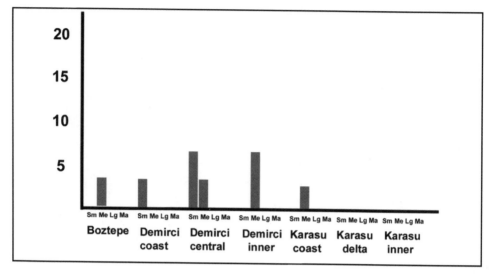

Figure 7-4: Byzantine and Seljuk settlement frequency on Boztepe and in the Demirci and Karasu valleys.

coasts were open to occasional raiding by Cossack pirates (Ostapchuk 1990), while villages set back from the coast were less exposed to such dangers.

Sinop in the Black Sea

We are now approaching the end of our journey through some of the places of the Sinop promontory. We have have attempted to trace the links and ruptures between many different times, places, and landscapes. But the history we are tracing here is dynamic and evolving. How far have we come in our exploration of this port and hinterland by the Hospitable Sea? Some remarkably persistent themes have emerged by synthesizing results of diverse research and reactions to Sinop over several thousand years. From at least the 7th century BCE and perhaps even earlier a port at Sinope controlled the crossroads of maritime communication through the Black Sea. At times close economic relationships between the port and the northern Black Sea or markets abroad prompted inhabitants to take advantage of the opportunities offered by the diverse landscapes of the promontory. At other times, the port's strategic position as a point for the transshipment of goods along the Black Sea Silk Route from Persian and Eurasian outlets like Trabzon and

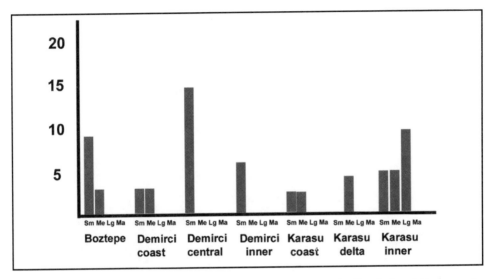

Figure 7-5: Ottoman settlement frequency on Boztepe and in the Demirci and Karasu valleys.

Caffa to Istanbul isolated the hinterland from the port and international markets.

Braudel (1972:25-102) begins his Mediterranean with the peninsulas and in particular, the mountains. Mountains, plateaus and plains are the leading actors in Braudel's structural history of the Mediterranean. The coasts and seas came next, and the complex variations of topography, ecology, and potential for communications structured patterns in human history that persisted through different political and cultural contexts. Braudel's mountains were suspended in a timeless poverty, the coasts and rivers a hubub of activity with cities and towns fed by the agricultural wealth of the plains. This continental scale of history champions continuities at the expense of local disruptions and discontinuities, the stuff of history and human experience (Horden and Purcell 2000:39–43, 463–66).

When places are considered on more intimate levels human actions condition subsequent behavior. In Sinop local contexts have been built on a succession of experiences, investments and uses. Changing political, economic, and cultural conditions molded and transformed the Sinop landscape: road systems, tensions of ethnic relationships, defensive architecture, and infrastructures of economic exploitation.

Far from the image of timeless isolation and poverty, the hinterland of Sinop has been a sensitive barometer of regional conditions over thousands of years. When tensions and rivalries have constricted Pontic interactions, the hinterland lay shadowed in poverty and isolation. However when complementary interests and needs have driven Black Sea connections, the hinterland has flourished through widespread engagement.

Epilogue:
Miles To Go

O ur survey and research by other colleagues in the Sinop region to
date allows us to start weaving stories about the landscapes, peo-
ples, and cultures of Sinop promontory, but we are a long way from the
end of our exploration. Many outstanding questions remain to be
addressed, and surely more will be encountered as we find ways to solve
existing puzzles. This brief epilogue sketches some of the larger outstanding issues that have emerged through our research and lays out
some of the ways in which we hope to address them.

Chronology and Typology

A firmly grounded chronology for local ceramic types needs to be established. This problem is particularly acute for prehistoric and post-
antique phases. We are undertaking a systematic program to date critical ware types in Sinop region using thermoluminescence (TL) dating.
TL dating has had a controversial history in archaeology, largely because
early attempts to use it did not take local soil composition into account.
Newer methods of data collection and analysis are making this method
more reliable for dating ceramics from excavated and surface contexts
(Dunnell et al. 1995).

We are also establishing ceramic typologies by a battery of physical
characterization processes, that will permit us to establish relationships
between local clay sources and ceramic production, and the develop-

ment and spread of technological and productive practices. Techniques such as neutron activation analysis (useful for clay sourcing), and Xeroradiography, ceramic petrography (both useful for understanding production and technology) will allow us to trace patterns of production and distribution in ceramic pottery and building materials.

Environment and Geomorphology

The development of the Sinop landscape and ecology needs to be clarified more extensively. Initial investigations in the Karasu delta area have been successful in tracing the development of that particular valley (Besonen et al. in preparation). Although important progress has been made, we are continuing to expand our coverage into different places in the promontory in a manner that complements our multi-sited focus. Furthermore, we will intensify our efforts to reconstruct the changing climate and floral communities of Sinop promontory through studies of pollen remains and surviving relict populations.

Particular Cultural Landscapes

At the outset we looked at how an archaeological landscape might in fact be a palimpsest of many different cultural landscapes. All the people of Sinop did not inhabit these landscapes in the same way, and we must be sensitive to these differences if we hope to explore them adequately. Several major issues have emerged as a result of examining these varied landscapes.

Precolonial Landscapes

Precolonial settlements in the region are frequently located in heavily forested places often ignored for agriculture in part because of their mounded forms. To date our quadrat sampling methodology, which surveys tracts areas with comparable visibility, has limited our ability to integrate the study of precolonial settlement with those of later periods. Transect samples will collect more continuous data from tracts with differing visibility. This will provide more reliable comparative data about the density and spatial organization of precolonial settlement through the promontory.

Colonial Landscapes

Sinope was a colony founded by the city of Miletus on the Aegean coast of Turkey. The structure of the hinterland landscapes of these two cities will be integrated through a coordinated study of field investigations and the results currently available. We will collaborate with the long-standing survey and excavation project at Sinope's founding city of Miletus to examine the development of the cultural, social, and economic hinterlands of a colonizing city and its colony.

Industrialized Landscapes

The industrial landscapes of the outer Sinop promontory have proven relatively well suited to the investigations conducted to date, but key questions remain with respect to these periods. First, our investigations have yet to yield sufficient evidence of sacred features in the Sinop landscape beyond the numerous cemeteries. Springs, woods, and other natural features often attracted the interests of Greeks and Romans, who saw them as imbued with sacred qualities. The emphasis on survey in high-visibility places may have limited our ability to integrate finds of sacred spaces that were concentrated in these kinds of marginal spaces. Furthermore, we have yet to explore the highland places of Sinop promontory in a systematic manner. Greeks and Romans frequently placed important sanctuaries in the caves and peaks of the highlands, and so, we are certainly missing this important part of Sinop's sacred landscape. In addition, the lack of systematic data from the highlands makes any models for understanding the economic relationships between these two kinds of places very tentative. A program of transect samples extending from the highlands to the coasts will help us to address these challenges. The ware characterization studies of pottery and building materials will prove invaluable in reconstructing economic relationships between these regions.

Post-antique Archaeology

New multidisciplinary studies of Byzantine, Seljuk, and Ottoman cultures by rigorous archaeological methods are placing post-antique archaeology (8th–20th centuries CE) among the most dynamic emerging disciplines in Anatolia. The rich documentation of infrastructure, economy and social life offered by Ottoman tax and court records has been vigorously exploited by text-oriented social historians for more than fifty years, but it has only recently become of interest to anthropologists and archaeologists. The landscape approach used by our survey to date has led to a number of difficulties in establishing comparable data sets. First and foremost, our emphasis on comparable visibility has neglected rigorous documentation of monuments within existing villages. Second, our discussions with local inhabitants have been relatively unstructured in the past, with little attempt to gather comparable social, cultural, economic, and historical data from all informants. Our field team now includes a full-time ethnohistorical group of anthropologists and architects who are recording and mapping data that can be integrated with the rich information from tax records and archaeological field results.

This work rightly brings our exploration of connection to the present day. The history of Sinop and its hinterland is the history of a multitude of different places linked in different ways depending on historical, economic, and cultural contexts. While many of these places have at times revisited former roles, such roles were produced and reproduced within dynamic frameworks. The green landscapes of Sinop charm visitors into thinking they wander through a timeless Eden (Figure 8-1). However remote the bustle of urban life may be from the daily experiences of the Sinop hinterland, its effects and connections pervade the lives of inhabitants. The older girl in Figure 8-1 is betrothed to a boy with whom she minded cattle and attended grade school in this village. He like many of the young men in these mountains now works in Istanbul. As they make their home there they are adding a bittersweet layer to the history of connection in Sinop.

Figure 8-1: Two village girls in the highlands of Sinop. Like most of the young people from the village these girls will move to Istanbul and other distant cities when they marry. The contributions they send home will sustain the older generation in this region where independent subsistence is no longer viable in the modern Turkish economy (courtesy of R. Olson).

Bibliography

Adams, R. McC. 1981. *Heartland of Cities*. Chicago, IL: University of Chicago Press.

Aelian. 1958. *On the Characteristics of Animals*. A. Schofield, ed., trans. Cambridge, MA: Harvard University Press.

Akkan, E. 1975. *Sinop Yarimadasinin Jeolomorfolojisi*. Ankara: Ankara Üniversityesi Dil ve Cografya Fakültesi Yayinlari.

Aksu, A., R. Hiscott, P. Mudie, A. Rochon, M. Kaminsky, T. Abrajano, and D. Yasar. 2002. "Persistent Holocene Outflow from the Black Sea to the Eastern Mediterranean Contradicts Noah's Flood Hypothesis." *GSA Today* 12,5:4–9.

Akurgal, E. 1956. "Sinop Kazilari" and "Die Ausgrabungen von Sinope." *Türk Arkeologi Dergesi* 6,1:47–61.

Akurgal, E., and L. Budde. 1956. *Vorläufiger Bericht über die Ausgrabungen in Sinope*. Ankara: Turk Tarihi Kurumu.

Alcock, S. 1993. *Graeca Capta: The Landscapes of Roman Greece*. Cambridge: Cambridge University Press.

———— 1994. "Minding the Gap in Hellenistic and Roman Greece." *In* S. Alcock and R. Osborne, eds., *Placing the Gods: Sanctuaries and Sacred Space in Ancient Greece*, 247–61. Oxford: Clarendon Press.

———— 2000. "Extracting Meaning from Ploughsoil Assemblages: Assessments of the Past, Strategies for the Future." *In* R. Francovich, H. Patterson, and G. Barker, eds., *The Archaeology of Mediterranean Landscapes*, 1–4. Oxford: Oxbow.

Alkim, U. B. 1975. "Samsun Bölgesi Çalismalari (1973)." *Türk Arkeologi Dergesi* 22:5–12.

Alkim, U. B., H. Alkim, and Ö. Bilgi. 1988. *Ikiztepe 1*. Ankara: Türk Tarihi Kurumu.

Appadurai, A. 1990. "Disjuncture and Difference in the Global Cultural Economy." *Public Culture* 2:1–24.

Arnaud, P. 1992. "Les Relations maritimes dans le Pont-Euxin d'apres le données numériques des géographes anciens." *Revue des etudes anciennes* 94:57–77.

Avram, A. 1999. "Materiel amphorique et non amphorique dans deux sites de la Chora d'Istros (Histria Pod et Cogealac)." *In* Y. Garlan, ed., *Production et Commerce des amphores anciennes en Mer Noire*, 215–30. Aix en Provence: Publications de l'Université de Provence.

——— 2001. "Les territoires d'Istros et de Callatis." *In* Convegno di studi sulla Magna Grecia, 2001, *Problemi della chora coloniale dall'Occidente al Mar Nero: atti del quarantesimo Convegno di studi sulla Magna Grecia, Taranto, 29 settembre–3 ottobre 2000*, 593–633. Taranto: Istituto per la storia e l'archeologia della Magna Grecia.

Ballance, S., A. Bryer, and D. Winfield. 1966. "Nineteenth-Century Monuments in the City and Vilayet of Trebizond: Architectural and Historical Notes, Part I." *Archeion Pontou* 28:233–308.

Ballard, R., F. Hiebert, D. Coleman, C. Ward, J. Smith, K. Willis, B. Foley, K. Croff, C. Major, and F. Torre. 2001. "Deepwater Archaeology of the Black Sea: The 2000 Season at Sinop, Turkey." *American Journal of Archaeology* 105:607–23.

Barker, G., ed. 1995. *A Mediterranean Valley*. London: Leicester University Press.

Barker, G., A. Grant, and T. Rasmussen. 1993. "Approaches to the Etruscan Landscape: The Development of the Tuscania Survey." *In* P. Bogucki ed., *Case Studies in European Prehistory*, 229–57. Boca Raton, FL: CRC.

Barker, G., and D. Mattingly. 1999–2000. *The Archaeology of Mediterranean Landscapes*. 5 vols. Oxford: Oxbow.

Barton, C. M., J. Bernabeu, J. E. Aura, L. Molina, and S. Schmich. 2001. "Historical Contingency, Nonlinearilty, and the Neolithization of the Western Mediterranean." Paper presented at the annual meeting of the Society of American Archaeology, New Orleans, April.

Bauer, A. 2001. "The Prehistoric Pottery of Sinop Province, Turkey: Observations on Pre-Greek Interaction in the Black Sea." Paper presented at the annual meeting of the Archaeological Institute of America, San Diego, 3–6 January.

———— 2002. "Between the Steppe and the Sown: Signs of Community in the Prehistoric Black Sea." Paper presented at the University of Chicago Eurasian Archaeology Conference, Beyond the Steppe and the Sown: Integrating Local and Global Visions, Chicago, 3–4 May.

Bauer, A., and O. Doonan. 2002. "Buying a Table in Erfelek: Some Thoughts on the Social Nature of Trade." Paper presented at the annual meeting of the Society for American Archaeology, Denver, April.

Belke, K. 1996. *Tabula Imperii Byzantini 9: Paphlagonien und Honorias Vienna*. Vienna: Verlag der österreichischen Akademie der Wissenschaften.

Bender, B. 1998. *Stonehenge. Making Space*. New York: Berg.

Bellér-Hann, I., and C. Hann. 2001. *Turkish Region: State, Market and Social Identities on the East Black Sea Coast*. Santa Fe, NM: SAR.

Bender, B., S. Hamilton, and C. Tilley. 2002. "Leskernick Homepage." Web page available at http://www.ucl.ac.uk/leskernick/home.htm.

Bilgi, Ö. 2001. "Ikiztepe kazilarinin 1999 dönemi sonuçlari." *Kazi Sonuçlari Toplantisi* 22:315–26.

———— forthcoming. *Ikiztepe 2*. Ankara: Türk Tarihi Kurumu.

Bintliff, J., P. Howard, and A. Snodgrass. 1999. "The Hidden Landscapes of Prehistoric Greece." *Journal of Mediterranean Archaeology* 12:139–68.

Bintliff, J., and A. Snodgrass. 1985. "The Cambridge/Bradford Boeotia Expedition: The First Four Years." *Journal of Field Archaeology* 12:123–61.

Boardman, J. 1990. "Early Greek Pottery on Black Sea Sites?" *Oxford Journal of Archaeology* 10:387–90.

Bourdieu, P. 1977. *Outline of a Theory of Practice*. Cambridge: Cambridge University Press.

Boysal, Y. 1959. "Über die Älteren Fünde von Sinope und die Kolonizationsfrage." *Archäologischer Anzeiger* :8–20.

Bradley, R. 2000. *An Archaeology of Natural Places*. London: Routledge.

Bratianu, G. 1969. *La Mer Noire*. Acta Historia 9. Munich: Societas Academica Dacoromana.

Braudel, F. 1972. *The Mediterranean and the Mediterranean World in Age of Philip II*. New York: William Collins' Sons.

Brunet, M., ed. 1999. *Territoires des cites greques*. Bulletin de Correspondance Hellénique, Supplement 34. Paris: Diffusion de Boccard.

Bryer, A. 1975. "Greeks and Türkmens: The Pontic Exception." *Dumbarton Oaks Papers* 29:113–49.

Bryer, A., and D. Winfield. 1985. *The Byzantine Monuments and Topography of the Pontos*. Dumbarton Oaks Studies 20. Washington, DC: Dumbarton Oaks.

Buck, C., W. Cavanagh, and C. Litton. 1995. *Bayesian Approach to Interpreting Archaeological Data*. Chichester: Wiley.

Budde, L. 1956. "Kurzer vorläufiger Bericht über die Grabungen in Sinope der Kampagnen 1951–1953." *Türk Arkeoloji Dergesi* 6,2:5–10.

——— 1963. "Eine Tierkampfgruppe aus Sinope." *Antike Plastik* 2:55–74.

Burney, C. 1956. "Northern Anatolia before Classical Times." *Anatolian Studies* 6:179–203.

Carter, J. C. 1983. *The Chora at Metapontum*. Austin, TX: University of Texas Press.

——— 2001. "La chora di Metaponto: risultati degli ultimi 25 anni di ricerca archeologica." *In* Convegno di studi sulla Magna Grecia 2001, *Problemi della chora coloniale dall'Occidente al Mar Nero: atti del quarantesimo Convegno di studi sulla Magna Grecia, Taranto, 29 settembre–3 ottobre 2000*, 771–92. Taranto: Istituto per la storia e l'archeologia della Magna Grecia.

Carter, J. C., M. Crawford, P. Lehman, G. Nikolaenko, and J. Trelogan. 2000. "The Chora of Chersonesos in Crimea, Ukraine." *American Journal of Archaeology* 104:707–41.

Cavanaugh, W., R. E. Jones, and A. E. Sarris. 1996. "The Phosphate Geophysical Surveys." *In* W. Cavanaugh, J. Crouwel, R. Catling, and G. Shipley, eds., *The Laconia Survey: Continuity and Change in a Greek Rural Landscape* 2, 235–62. British School of Archaeology at Athens, Supplement 27. London: British School at Athens.

Cherry, J. 1982. "A Preliminary Definition of Site Distribution on Melos." *In* C. Renfrew and M. Wagstaff, eds., *An Island Polity: The Archaeology of Exploitation in Melos*, 10–23. Cambridge: Cambridge University Press.

———— 1994. "Regional Survey in the Mediterranean: The 'New Wave' (And After)." *In* P. N. Kardulias, ed., *Beyond the Site: Regional Studies in the Aegean Area*, 91–112. New York: University Press of America.

Cherry, J., J. Davis, and E. Mantzourani. 1991. *Landscape Archaeology as Long-term History*. Monumenta Archaeologica 16. Los Angeles: UCLA Institute of Archaeology.

Clavio. 1928. *Embassy to Tamerlane, 1403-1406*. G. Le Stange trans., London: Routledge.

Clifford, J. 1994. "Diasporas." *Cultural Anthropology* 9:302–38.

Convegno di studi sulla Magna Grecia. 2001. *Problemi della chora coloniale dall'Occidente al Mar Nero: atti del quarantesimo Convegno di studi sulla Magna Grecia, Taranto, 29 settembre–3 ottobre 2000*. Taranto: Istituto per la storia e l'archeologia della Magna Grecia.

Conovici, N. 1998. *Histria 8. Les timbres amphoriques, 2. Sinope*. Paris: Diffusion de Boccard.

Cowgill, G. 1990. "Toward Refining Concepts of Full-Coverage Survey." *In* S. Fish and S. Kowalewski, eds., *The Archaeology of Regions*, 249–59. Washington, DC: Smithsonian Institution Press.

Crumley, C. 1995. "Heterarchy and the Analysis of Complex Societies." *In* R. Erenreich, C. Crumley, and J. Levy, eds., *Heterarchy and the Analysis of Complex Societies*. Arlington, VA: Archaeological Papers of the American Anthropological Association 6.

Davis, J., ed. 1998. *Sandy Pylos*. Austin, TX: University of Texas Press.

Davis, P. 1965. *Flora of Turkey and the East Aegean Islands*. 1. Edinburgh: Edinburgh University Press.

de Boer, J. 2001. "Sinopean Amphora Stamps on the Northern and Western Black Sea Coasts." *In* S. Solovyev and G. Tsetskhladze, eds., *Taman Antiquity 3: Greeks and Natives in the Cimmerian Bosphorus*, 132–33. St. Petersburg: State Hermitage Museum.

Deetz, J. 1990. "Landscapes as Cultural Statements." *In* W. Kelso and R. Most, eds., *Earth Patterns*, 1–4. Charlottesville, VA: University Press of Virginia.

Dengate, J. 1978. "A Site Survey along the South Shore of the Black Sea." *In* E. Akurgal, ed., *Proceedings of the Tenth International Conference of Classical Archaeology (Ankara)*, 245–58. Ankara: Türk Tarih Kurumu.

Dereli, F., and Y. Garlan. 1997. "Quelques nouvelles amphores timbrees de Sinope." *Anatolia Antiqua* 5:199–209.

Dönmez, S. 1999. "Sinop'ta çanti yapilar." *Arredamento Mimarlik* 100:12–14.

Doonan, O. 1998. "Sinop Regional Survey, 1996–97." *Near Eastern Archaeologist* 1:178–79.

——— 2001. "Sampling Sinop: Putting Together the Pieces of a Fragmented Landscape." Paper presented at the annual meeting of the Society of American Archaeology, New Orleans.

——— 2002. "Production in a Pontic Landscape: The Hinterland of Greek and Roman Sinope." *In* M. Faudot, A. Fraysse, and E. Geny, eds., *Pont-Euxin et Commerce: La genèse de la "Route de soie,"* 185–98. Actes du Ixe Symposium de Vani. Besançon: Presses Universitaires Franc-Comtoises.

——— 2003. "Sinope." *In* D. Grammenos and E. Petropoulos, eds., *Ancient Greek Colonies in the Black Sea, 1379–1403.* Archaeological Institute of Northern Greece 4. Thessaloniki: Altintzis.

——— In press. "Colony and Conjuncture: the Early Greek Colony at Sinope." *In Frühes Ionien: Eine Bestandaufsnahme.* Milesische Forschungen. Mainz am Rhein: von Zabern.

Doonan, O., and A. Gantos. In preparation a. "Systematic Survey in the Demirci Valley, Sinop, Turkey."

——— In preparation b. "Sinope Colonia Sitiens: A Note on Pliny, Ep. X.xc-xci based on Recent Results of the Sinop Regional Survey."

Doonan, O., A. Gantos, and F. Hiebert. 1998. "Survey of Sinop Province, Turkey." *American Journal of Archaeology* 102:367.

——— 1999. "Sinop Ili Systematik Yüzey *Arastirmasi 1997."* *Arastirma Sonuçlari Toplantisi* 16:359–71.

Doonan, O., A. Gantos, F. Hiebert, A. Yaycioglu, and M. Besonen. 1999. "Sinop Bölgesel Arkeoloji Arastirmasi 1998: Karasu Vadi Arastirmasi." *Arastirma Sonuçlari Toplantisi* 17:345–56.

——— 2000. "Sinop Ili Systematik Yüzey Arastirmasi 1999: Karasu Vadi Arastirmasi." *Arastirma Sonuçlari Toplantisi* 18:345–56.

——— 2001. "Sinop Regional Survey 1998–1999: The Karasu Valley Survey." *TüBA-AR* 4:113–35.

Doonan, O., and D. Smart. 2000–2001. "Gerna, Sinop and Roman-Byzantine Settlement along the Coast West of Sinop." *Talanta* 32–33:17–24.

Dougherty, C. 1993. *The Poetics of Colonization.* Oxford: Oxford University Press.

Drahor, M., A. Hesse, and M. Kaya. 1995. "Sinop Amfora Atölyeleri Manyetik Çalismalar." *Jeofizik* 9,10:7–12.

Dunnell, R. 1992. "The Notion Site." *In* J. Rossignol and L. Wandsnider, eds., *Time, Space and Archaeological Landscapes,* 21–41. New York: Plenum.

Dunnell, R. C., and J. Feathers. 1995. "Thermoluminescence Dating of Surficial Archaeological Material." *In* C. Beck, ed., *Dating in Surface Context,* 115–37. Albuquerque, NM: University of New Mexico Press.

Erzen, A. 1956. "Sinop Kazisi 1953 Yili Çalismalari." *Türk Arkeoloji Dergesi* 6,1:69–72.

Faroqhi, S. 1984. *Towns and Townsmen of Ottoman Anatolia.* Cambridge: Cambridge University Press.

——— 1997. "Sinub 2. The Ottoman and Modern Periods." *In* C. Bosworth, ed. *The Encyclopedia of Islam,* 654–56. Leiden: E. J. Brill.

Fedoseev, N. 1992. "Itogi i perspektivy izucheniya sinopskih keramicheskih kleim (Conclusions and perspectives on the study of pottery stamps from Sinope)." *In* V. Kats and S. Monakhov, eds., *Grecheskie amphory.* Saratov: Izdatel'stvo Saratovskogo universiteta.

——— 1999. "Classification des timbres astynomiques de Sinope." *In* Y. Garlan, ed., *Production et Commerce des amphores anciennes en Mer Noire,* 27–48. Aix en Provence: Publications de l'Université de Provence.

Fentress, E. 2001. "Villas, Wine and Kilns: the Landscape of Jerba in the Late Hellenistic Period." *Journal of Roman Archaeology* 14,1:249–68.

Fish, S., and S. Kowalewski, eds. 1990. *The Archaeology of Regions. A Case for Full Coverage Survey.* Washington, DC: Smithsonian Institution Press.

Foss, P. 2001. "GPS, GIS and WWW in Archaeological Survey Comparability." Paper presented at the annual meeting of the Society of American Archaeology, New Orleans, April.

French, D. 1981; 1988b. *Roman Roads and Milestones of Asia Minor,* 2 vols. BAR International Series 392. Oxford: BAR.

———— 1984. "Classis Pontica." *Epigraphica Anatolica* 4:53–59.

———— 1985a. "Sinope and the Thracian Coast." *Thracia Pontica* 2:85–88.

———— 1985b. "Bythinian Troops in the Kingdom of the Bosphorus." *Epigraphica Anatolica* 6:97–102.

———— 1986. "Stephane. *Anadolu Arastirmalari* 10:483–98.

———— 1988. "Non-Greek Names at Sinope." *In* I. Kazluzhskaya, ed., *Etnogenez narodov Iugo-Vostochnoi Evropy* 57. Moscow: Institut Slavyanovedenya y Balkanistiki.

———— 1990. "Sinopean Notes 1." *Epigraphica Anatolica* 16: 45–64.

———— 1991a. "The Iron Age in the Black Sea." *Thracia Pontica* 4: 237–40.

———— 1991b. "Sinopean Notes 2." *Epigraphica Anatolica* 18: 141–56.

———— 1991c. "New Milestones from Pontus and Galatia." *In* B. Remy, ed., *Pontica* 1, 77–96. Istanbul: Isis yayincilik.

———— 1992. "Sinopean Notes 3." *Epigraphica Anatolica* 19:45–60.

———— 1994a. "Sinopean Notes 5." *Epigraphica Anatolica* 23:109–12.

———— 1994b. "Sinopean Notes 4. Cults and Divinities, the Epigraphic Evidence." *Epigraphica Anatolica* 23:99–108.

Garlan, Y. 1990. "Remarques sur les timbres amphoriques du Sinope." *Comptes Rendus de séances de l'Accadémie des inscriptions et belles letters* :490–507.

Garlan, Y., ed. 1999. *Production et Commerce des amphores anciennes en Mer Noire*. Aix en Provence: Publications de l'Université de Provence.

Garlan, Y., and D. Kassab Tezgör. 1996. "Prospection d'ateliers d'amphores et de Ceramiques de Sinope." *Anatolia Antiqua* 4:325–34.

Garlan, Y., and I. Tatlican. 1997a. "1994 ve 1995 Yillari Zeytinlik (Sinop) Amphora Atölyeri Kazisi." *Kazi Sonuçlari Toplantisi* 18:337–51.

———— 1997b. "Fouilles d'ateliers amphoriques a Zeytinlik (Sinop) en 1994 et 1995." *Anatolia Antiqua* 5:307–16.

———— "Fouilles d'ateliers amphoriques a Nisiköy et a Zeytinlik (Sinop) en 1996 et 1997." *Anatolia Antiqua* 6:407–22.

Gibb, H., trans. 1962. *The Travels of Ibn Battutah* 2. Cambridge: Cambridge University Press.

Gillings, M., and K. Sbonias. 1999. "Regional Survey and GIS: The Boeotia Project." *In* M. Gillings, D. Mattingly, and J. van Dalen, eds., *Geographical Information Systems and Landscape Archaeology*, 35–54. Oxford: Oxbow.

Given, M. 2001. "From Density Counts to Ideational Landscapes: Intensive Survey, Landscape Archaeology and the Sydney Cyprus Survey Project." Paper presented at the annual meeting of the Society of American Archaeology, New Orleans, April.

Graham, A. J. 1983. "The Colonial Expansion of Greece." *In Cambridge Ancient History* 3,3, 83–162. Cambridge: Cambridge University Press.

Gurney, O. 1990. *The Hittites* 4th ed. New York: Penguin.

Hall, J. 1997. *Ethnic Identity in Greek Antiquity*. Cambridge: Cambridge University Press.

Hamilton, W. 1842. *Researches in Asia Minor*. London: John Murray.

Harrison, T., and S. Batiuk. 2001. "The 1999 Amuq Valley Regional Project Survey." *Arastirma Sonuçlari Toplantisi* 18:181–86.

Hiebert, F. 2001. "Black Sea Coastal Cultures: Trade and Interaction." *Expedition* 43:11–20.

Hiebert, F., O. Doonan, and J. Smith. In preparation. *Sinop Kale Northwest Excavations, 2000*.

Hiebert, F., D. Smart, A. Gantos, and O. Doonan. 1997. "From Mountaintop to Ocean Bottom: A Holistic Approach to Archaeological Survey along the Turkish Black Sea Coast." *In* J. Tancredi, ed., *Ocean Pulse*, 93–108. New York: Plenum.

Hill, S. 1995. "The first season of rescue excavations at Çiftlik (Sinop)." *Anatolian Studies* 45:219–32.

―――― 1998. "Çiftlik." *Anatolian Archaeology* 4:6–7.

―――― 1999. "Rescue Excavations at Çiftlik (Sinop)." *In* R. Matthews, ed., *Ancient Anatolia. Fifty Years' Work by the British Institute of Archaeology at Ankara*, 285–300. Ankara: British Institute of Archaeology at Ankara.

Hind, J. 1988. "The Colonisation of Sinope and the South-East Black Sea Area." *In* O. Lordkipanidze, ed., *Local Ethno-political Entities of the Black Sea Area in the 7th-4th Centuries B.C.*, 207–23. Tbilisi: Metsniereba.

―――― 1995–96. "Traders and Ports of Trade (Emporoi and Emporia) in the Black Sea in Antiquity." *Il Mare Nero* II:113–26.

Hodder, I., and C. Orton. 1976. *Spatial Analysis in Archaeology.* Cambridge: Cambridge University Press.

Hodder, I. 1986. *Reading the Past.* Cambridge: Cambridge University Press.

Hodder, I., ed. 2000. *Towards Reflexive Method in Archaeology: The Example at Çatalhöyük.* Ankara: British Institute of Archaeology at Ankara.

Hommaire de Hell, X. 1860. *Voyage en Turquie et en Perse exécuté per ordre de Gouvernement Français pendent les anneés 1846, 1847, 1848.* Paris: P. Bertrand Libraire-éditeur.

Horden, P., and N. Purcell. 2000. *The Corrupting Sea.* Oxford: Blackwell.

Inalcik, H. 1995. *The Customs Register of Caffa, 1487–1490.* Sources and Studies on the Ottoman Black Sea I. Cambridge, MA: Department of Near Eastern Languages and Literatures, Harvard University.

Isin, M. A. 1989. *Sinop.* Ankara: Dönmez Offset.

———— 1990. "Sinop Bölgesi Yüzey Arastirmasi." *In* M. Saglam, ed., *Ikinci Tarih Boyunca Karadeniz Kongresi Bildirileri,* 241–76. Samsun: Ondokuz Mayis Üniversitesi Egitim Fakültesi.

———— 1991. "Kocagöz Höyük'te bulunan tek kupla kuplalar." *Türk Arkeoloji Dergesi* 29:177–91.

———— 1998. "Sinop Region Field Survey." *Anatolia Antiqua* 6:95–139.

Ivantchik, A. 1998. "Die Gründung von Sinope und die Probleme der Anfangsphase der griechischen Kolonisation des Schwarz-meergebiets." *In* G. Tsetskhladze, ed., *The Colonisation of the Black Sea Area,* 297–330. Stuttgart: Franz Steiner Verlag.

———— 2001. "The State of the Cimmerian Problem." *Ancient Civilizations Scythia to Siberia* 7:307–39.

Jones, C. 1988. "A Monument from Sinope." *Journal of Hellenic Studies* 108:193–94.

Kacharava, D. 1997. "The Greco-Kolkhian Trade Connections in the 7th-4th centuries BC." *In* J. Fossey, ed., *Proceedings of the First International Conference on the Archaeology and History of the Black Sea,* 137–46. Amsterdam: Gieben.

Kardulias, P. N., ed. 1994a. *Beyond the Site: Regional Studies in the Aegean Area.* New York: University Press of America.

Kardulias, P. N. 1994b. "Paradigms of the Past in Greek Archaeology" *In* P. N. Kardulias, ed., *Beyond the Site: Regional Studies in the Aegean Area*. New York: University Press of America.

Kassab Tezgör, D. 1996. "Fouilles des ateliers d'amphores a Demirci pres de Sinope en 1994 et 1995." *Anatolia Antiqua* 4:335–54.

———— 1999. "Sinope et le commerce de ses amphores." *Dziebani. Journal of the Centre for Archaeological Studies of the Georgian Academy of Sciences* 1:54–55.

Kassab Tezgör, D., and I. Tatlican. 1997. "Sinop-Demirci Anfora Atölyerinin 1995 Kazisi." *Kazi Sonuçlari Toplantisi* 18:353–65.

———— 1998. "Fouilles des ateliers d'amphores a Demirci." *Anatolia Antiqua* 6:423–42.

Keay, S. 2000. "Ceramic Chronology and Roman Rural Settlement in the Lower Guadalquivir Valley." *In* R. Francovich, H. Patterson, and G. Barker, eds., *Extracting Meaning from Ploughsoil Assemblages*, 162–73. Oxford: Oxbow.

Kiepert, R. 1902–06. *Karte von Kleinasien*. Berlin: Dietrich Reiner.

Kiziltan, Z. 1991. "Samsun Bölgesi Yüzey Arastirmalari 1971-1977." *Belleten* 56:213–42.

Knapp, A. B., and W. Ashmore. 1999. "Archaeological Landscapes: Constructed, Conceptualized, Ideational." *In* W. Ashmore and A. B. Knapp, eds., *Archaeologies of Landscape*, 1-30. Oxford: Blackwell.

Knudsen, S. 1995. "Fisheries along the Eastern Black Sea Coast of Turkey: Informal Resource Management in Small-scale Fishing in the Shadow of a Dominant Capitalist Fishery." *Human Organization* 54:437–48.

Kuniholm, P. 2000. "Dendrochronologically dated Ottoman monuments." *In* U. Baram and L. Carroll, eds., *A Historical Archaeology of the Ottoman Empire*, 93–136. New York: Plenum.

Kuzucuoglu, C., and A. Andrieu. 1998. "Les ateliers de Demirci (Sinop): Approche geomorphologique du site et premier elements de response analytiques." *Anatolia Antiqua* 6:451–56.

Kuzucuoglu, C., C. Marro, A. Özdogan and A. Tibet. 1997. "Prospection archeologique franco-turque dans la region de Kastamonu (Mer Noire). Deuxieme Rapport Preliminaire." *Anatolia Antiqua* 5:275–306.

Ladas, S. 1932. *The Exchange of Minorities Bulgaria, Greece and Turkey*. New York: Macmillan.

Langella, A. 1989. "Sinope, Datame e la Persia." *Dialoghi di Archeologia* 7.2:93–107.

Leaf, W. 1916. "The Commerce of Sinop." *Journal of Hellenic Studies* 36:1–15.

Llobera, M. 2001. "Building Past Landscape Perception with GIS: Understanding Topographic Prominence." *Journal of Archaeological Science* 28:1005–14.

Lohmann, H. 1999. "Survey in der chora von Milet: Vorbericht über die Kampagnen der Jahre 1996 und 1997." *Archäologischer Anzeiger* 1999:439–73.

Lordkipanidze, O. 1979. *Problemy grecheskoi kolonizatsii Severnogo i Vostochnogo Prichernomor'ia: materialy I Vsesoiuznogo simpoziuma po drevnei istorii Prichernomor'ia, TSkhaltubo, 1977.* Tbilisi: Metsniereba.

Maksimova, M. 1956. *Antichniye Goroda Iugo-Vostochnogo Prichernomorya. Sinopa, Amis, Trapezunt.* Moscow: Institute for Historical Material Culture.

Marcus, G. 1995. "Ethnography in/of the World System: The Emergence of Multi-sited Ethnography." *Annual Review of Anthropology* 24:95–117.

Marek, C. 1993. *Stadt, Ära und Territorium in Pontus-Bithynia und Nord-Galatia.* Istanbuler Forschungen Bd. 39. Tübingen: E. Wasmuth.

Marro, C., A. Özdogan, and A. Tibet. 1996. "Prospection archeologique franco-turque dans la region de Kastamonu (Mer Noire). Premier Rapport Preliminaire." *Anatolia Antiqua* 4:273–90.

Matthews, R. 2001. "Project Paphlagonia: Regional Survey in Çankiri and Karabük Provinces, 1999." *Arastirma Sonuçlari Toplantisi* 18:249–56.

Matthews, R., T. Pollard, and M. Ramage. 1999. "Project Paphlagonia: Regional Survey in Northern Anatolia." *In* R. Matthews, ed., *Ancient Anatolia*, 195–206. Ankara: British Institute of Archaeology at Ankara.

Mattingly, D. 1988. "Oil for export? A comparison of Libyan, Spanish and Tunisian olive oil production in the Roman Empire." *Journal of Roman Archaeology* 1:33–56.

——— 1992. "The Field Survey: Strategy, Methodology and Preliminary results." *In* N. Ben Lazreg and D. Mattingly, eds., *Leptiminus (Lamta). A Roman Port City in Tunisia. Report No. 1,*

89–114. Supplement 4. Ann Arbor: Journal of Roman Archaeology.

—— 2000. "Methods of Collection, Recording and Quantification." *In* R. Francovich, H. Patterson, and G. Barker, eds., *The Archaeology of Mediterranean Landscapes*, 5–15. Oxford: Oxbow.

Mattingly, H. 1989. "Athens and the Black Sea in the Fifth Century B.C." *In* O. Lordkipanidze, ed., *Sur les traces des Argonauts*, 151–57. Paris: Annales Littéraires de l'Université de Besançon.

McGlade, J. 1999. "Archaeology and the Evolution of Cultural Landscapes: Towards an Interdisciplinary Research Agenda." *In* P. Ucko and R. Layton, eds., *The Archaeology and Anthropology of Landscape*, 458–82. London: Routledge.

Meeker, M. E. 1971. "The Black Sea Turks: Some Aspects of their Ethnic and Cultural Background." *International Journal of Middle East Studies* 2:318–45.

—— 2002. *A Nation of Empire: The Ottoman Legacy of Turkish Modernity*. Berkeley, CA: University of California Press.

Melber, J., ed. 1970. *Polyaeni Stategematon Libri Octo*. Stuttgart: B. G. Teubner.

Mitchell, S. 1993. *Anatolia. Land, Men and Gods in Asia Minor*. Oxford: Clarendon.

Monachov, S. 1993. "Les amphores de Sinope." *Anatolia Antiqua* 2:107–32.

Moreau, J. 1959. "Sur une inscription du Sinope." *In Limesstudien. Vorträge des 3. International Limes-Kongresses in Rheinfelden und Basel*, 84–87. Basel: Verlag der Institut für Ur- und Frühgeschichte der Schweiz.

Mueller, C., ed. 1855. *Geographi Graeci Minores*. Paris: Didot Brothers.

Munro, J. 1901. "Roads in Pontus, Royal and Roman." *Journal of Hellenic Studies* 21:52–66.

Murray, P., and P. N. Kardulias. 1988. "A Modern Site Survey in the Southern Argolid, Greece." *Journal of Field Archaeology* 13:21–41.

Ostapchuk, V. 1990. "An Ottoman Gaziname on Halil Pasha's Naval Campaign against the Cossacks." *Harvard Ukrainian Studies* 14:482–506.

Otten, H. 1973. *Eine althethische Erzählung um die Stadt Zalpa*. Wiesbaden: O. Harrassowitz.

Özgen, I. 2002. "The Hacimusalar Project: A Multidisciplinary Archaeological Project in Southwestern Turkey." Web site available at http://www.choma.org.

Özveren, E. 1997. "A Framework for the Study of the Black Sea World, 1789–1915." *Review* 20:77–113.

———— 2001. "The Black Sea as a Unit of Analysis." *In* T. Aybak, ed., *Politics of the Black Sea: Dynamics of Cooperation and Conflict*, 61–84. London: I. B. Tauris.

Peacock, D., F. Bejaoui, and N. Ben Lazreg. 1990. "Roman Pottery Production in Central Tunisia." *Journal of Roman Archaeology* 3:59–84.

Plog, F. 1990. "Some Thoughts on Full-Coverage Surveys." *In* S. Fish and S. Kowalewski, eds., *The Archaeology of Regions*, 243–47. Washington, DC: Smithsonian Institution Press.

Price, R. 1993. "The West Pontic Maritime Interaction Sphere: A Long-term Structure in Balkan Prehistory?" *Oxford Journal of Archaeology* 12:175–96.

Rauh, N. 2002. "Rough Cilicia Archaeological Survey Project." Web site available at http://pasture.ecn.purdue.edu/~rauhn/openingpage.htm

Rauh, N., and K. Slane 2000. "Possible Amphora Kiln Sites in West Rough Cilicia." *Journal of Roman Archaeology* 13,1:319–30.

Roberts, N., C. Kuzucuoglu, and M. Karabiyikoglu, eds. 1999. "The Late Quaternary in the Eastern Mediterranean Region." *Quaternary Science Reviews* 18, 4–5:497–716.

Robinson, D. 1906. "Ancient Sinope." *American Journal of Philology* 27:125–53, 245–79.

———— 1905. "Greek and Latin Inscriptions from Sinope and Environs." *American Journal of Archaeology* 9:294–333.

Romano, D. 1998. "GIS Based Analysis of Ancient Land Division in the Corinthia, Greece." *In* B. Slapsak, Z. Stancic, and J. Peterson, eds., *The Use of Geographic Information Systems in the Study of Ancient Landscapes and Features Related to Ancient Land Use*, 21–30. Brussels: Office for Official Publications of the European Communities.

Roodenberg, J., ed. 1995. *The Ilipinar Excavations* I. Istanbul: Nederlands Historisch-Archaeologisch Instituut te Istanbul.

Ryan, W., W. Pitman III, C. Major, K. Shimkus, V. Moskalenko, G. Jones, P. Dimitrov, N. Gorur, M. Sakinc, and H. Yuce. 1997.

"An Abrupt Drowning of the Black Sea Shelf." *Marine Geology* 138:119–26.

Sayre, E., E. Joel, M. Blackmann, K. A. Yener, and H. Özbal. 2001. "Stable Lead Isotope Studies of Black Sea Anatolian Ore Sources and Related Bronze Age and Phrygian Artefacts from Nearby Archaeological Sites. Appendix: New Central Taurus Ore Data." *Archaeometry* 43:77–115.

Scholl, T., and V. Zinko. 1999. *Archaeological Map of Nymphaion (Crimea)*. Warsaw: Institute of Archaeology and Ethnology.

Schortman, E., and P. Urban. 1994. "Current Trends in Interaction Research." *In* E. Schortman and P. Urban, eds., *Resources, Power and Interregional Interaction*, 235–55. New York: Plenum.

Sekunda, K. 1988. "Some Notes on the Life of Datames." *Iran* 26:35–53.

Shami, S. 2000. "Prehistories of Globalization: Circassian Identity in Motion." *Public Culture* 12:177–204.

Shcheglov, A. 1992. *Polis et Chora*. Besançon, Annales Littéraires de Besançon 476. Paris: Diffusion des Belles Lettres.

Sinop Valiligi. 2002. Sinop Provincial Government website. available at http://www.sinop.gov.tr/

Solovyov, S. 1999. *Ancient Berezan*. Colloquia Pontica 4. Leiden: E. J. Brill.

———— 2001. "On the History of the City-States in the Lower Bug Area: Borysthenes and Olbia." *In* J. Boardman, S. Solovyov, and G. Tsetskhladze, eds., *Northern Pontic Antiquities in the State Hermitage Museum*, 113–25. Colloquia Pontica 7. Leiden: E. J. Brill.

Speidel, M., and D. French. 1985. "Bithynian Troops in the Kingdom of Pontus." *Epigraphica Anatolica* 6:97–102.

Spencer, N. 1998. "History of Archaeological Investigations in Messina." *In* J. Davis, ed., *Sandy Pylos*, 23–41. Austin, TX: University of Texas Press.

Stein, G. 1999. *Rethinking World-systems: Diasporas, Colonies, and Interaction in Uruk Mesopotamia*. Tucson, AZ: University of Arizona Press.

Steinhauser, F. 1970. *Climatic Atlas of Europe*. Geneva: World Meteorological Organization.

Stone, D., L. Stirling, and N. Ben Lazreg. 1998. "Suburban Land-use and Ceramic Production around Leptiminus (Tunisia):

Interim Report." *Journal of Roman Archaeology* 11: 305–17.

Stoop, M. 1977–78. "Ancient Armene and its Harbor." *Anatolica* 6:117–24.

Strabo. 1960. *Geography*. H. Jones, ed., trans. Cambridge, MA: Harvard University Press.

Sumner, W. 1990. "Full-Coverage Regional Archaeological Survey in the Near East: An Example from Iran." *In* S. Fish and S. Kowalewski, eds., *The Archaeology of Regions*, 87–115. Washington, DC: Smithsonian Institution Press.

Surikov, I. 2001. "Historico-Geographical Questions Cennected with Pericles' Pontic Expedition." *Ancient Civilizations Scythia to Siberia* 7:341–66.

Tafur. 1926. *Travels and Adventures, 1435-1439*. M. Letts trans., New York: Harper.

Tarkan, H. 1941. *Sinop Cografyasi*. Izmir: Marifet matbasi.

Tatlican, I. 1997. "Sinop Çiftlik köyü, Mozaik Kurtarma Kazisi." *Müze Kurtarma Kazilari Semineri* 7:333–56.

Terrace, E. 1963. "Two Achaemenian Objects in the Boston Museum of Fine Arts." *Antike Kunst* 6:72–80.

Theophrastus. 1948. *Enquiry into Plants*. A. Hort ed., trans. Cambridge, MA: Harvard University Press.

Tilley, C. 1994. *A Phenomenology of Landscape*. Oxford: Berg.

Tsetskhladze, G. 1998. "Greek Colonisation of the Black Sea Area: Stages, Models and Native Population." *In* G. Tsetskhladze, ed., *The Greek Colonisation of the Black Sea Area*, 9–68. Historia Einzelschriften 121. Stuttgart: F. Steiner Verlag.

———— 1999. *Pichvnari and its Environs*. Paris: Annales Littéraires de l'Université de Franche-Comté, 659.

Tsetskhladze, G., and M. Triester. 1995. "The Metallurgy and Production of Precious Metals in Colchis before and after the Arrival of the Ionians." *Bulletin of the Metals Museum* 24:1–32.

Tsetskhladze, G., and S. Vnukov. 1992. "Colchian Amphorae: Typology, Chronology and Aspects of Production." *Annual of the British School at Athens* 87:357–86.

Vinogradov, IU. 1997. "Die politische Verfassung von Sinope und Olbia im fünften Jahrhundert v.u.Z." *In* IU. Vinogradov, ed., *Pontische Studien*, 165–229. Mainz: von Zabern.

Vinogradov, IU., and S. Kryzhitskii. 1995. *Olbia: eine altgriechische Stadt im nordwestlichen Schwarzmeerraum.* Leiden: E. J. Brill.

Vnukov, S. 1993. "New types of the Late Sinope Amphorae" (in Russian). *Rossiskaya Arkhaeologiya* 3:204–13.

―――― 1994. "The Comparative and Petrological Analysis of Sinope Amphorae" (in Russian). *Bosporskii Sbornik* 4:24–31.

Waelkens, M., and L. Loots. 2000. *Sagalassos V: Report on the Survey and Excavation Campaigns of 1996 and 1997.* Leuven: Leuven University Press.

Wandsnider, L. 1998. "Regional Scale Processes and Archaeological Landscape Units." *In* A. Ramenofsky and A. Steffen, eds., *Unit Issues in Archaeology,* 87–102. Salt Lake City, UT: University of Utah Press.

Wandsnider, L., N. Rauh, M. Hoff, R. Townsend, M. Dillon, and F. S. Özaner. 2001. "Artifact and Temporality: Tracking the Human-Natural System in Roman Era Western Rough Cilicia." Paper presented at annual meeting of the Society of American Archaeology, New Orleans, April.

Wascowicz, A. 1975. *Olbia Pontique et son Territoire.* Besançon: Annales Lettéraires de L'Université de Besançon, 168.

Westerdahl, C. 2001. "The Maritime Cultural Landscape: On the Concept of the Traditional Zones of Transport Geography." Website available on-line at http://www.abc.se/~m10354/publ/cult-land.htm

Wilkinson, T. 2000. "Regional Approaches to Mesopotamian Archaeology: The Contribution of Archaeological Surveys." *Journal of Archaeological Research* 8:219–67.

Wilson, D. 1960. "The Historical Geography of Bithynia, Paphlagonia and Pontus in the Greek and Roman Periods: A New Survey with Particular Reference to Surface Remains still Visible." B.Litt. thesis, Oxford University.

Winterhalder, B. 1994. "Concepts in Historical Ecology: The View from Evolutionary Theory." *In* C. Crumley, ed., *Historical Ecology,* 17–41. Santa Fe, NM: SAR.

Wright, J., J. Cherry, J. Davis, E. Mantzourani, S. Sutton, and R. Sutton. 1990. "The Nemea Valley Archaeological Project: A Preliminary Report." *Hesperia* 59:579–659.

von Gall, H. 1966. *Die Paphlagonischen Felsgraber.* Istanbuler Mitteilungen Beiheft 1. Tübingen: Wasmuth.

Index